Dear Kelly,

Thank you for being such a wonderful friend and advocate for what I am doing. I am very lucky to have met you!

All my best

Nick

THE TRUTH SHALL SET YOUR WALLET FREE

NICHOLAS W. STULLER

POST HILL
PRESS

A POST HILL PRESS BOOK
ISBN: 978-1-68261-775-5
ISBN (eBook): 978-1-68261-776-2

The Truth Shall Set Your Wallet Free:
Secrets to Finding the Perfect Financial Advisor
© 2018 by Nicholas W. Stuller
All Rights Reserved

Post Hill Press
New York • Nashville
posthillpress.com

Published in the United States of America

To my wife Kara for her amazing understanding, patience and support

To my daughter Tallulah for her unconditional love

CONTENTS

INTRODUCTION

Billionaires, millionaires, middle class, and anyone in financial distress can benefit by reading this book. I have attempted to provide a thorough education on the financial advisor universe, with information that can help everyone—regardless of their income or asset levels—find an ideal financial advisor. For those who have never hired an advisor, you will get the most benefit from "The Truth." If you have an advisor but are uncertain about how best to work together, you will learn more about how advisors work and you'll be better prepared to ask deeper questions. Even if you are well-versed in how advisors work, you will still discover some valuable nuggets to improve the results from your advisor relationship.

I have been in the financial services industry for more than thirty years and every year, it becomes more apparent to me that consumers desperately need financial advisors. The financial world becomes increasingly complex—and yet, consumers' knowledge of advisors does not seem to change much. Investors seem to make the exact same mistakes year in and year out, and less than half of Americans use a financial advisor. In my opinion, that's far too low a number. For a point of clarity, throughout the book I use the terms "consumer" and "investor" in what may appear to be an interchangeable basis. My use of consumer relates to someone who doesn't yet invest, but needs some kind of advice—usually a financial plan or some discrete advice as part of a plan. An investor is someone who is currently investing in some type of securities.

The subtitle of the book has the word "perfect" in it. For purposes of the book, "perfect" is defined as perfect for you at this time in your life. Advisors are people, and as such, will and do make mistakes. Your perfect financial advisor at this time in your life may very well be a bad fit for someone else, and vice versa. Financial advice is a mix of art and science; therefore, the human interaction component is important. As I explain in this book, if you are given the best advice ever known to man, but you do not use that advice for one reason or another, the advice is useless. The message, the messenger, and the recipient all have important roles in the advice dynamic.

I firmly believe every adult in the United States should get a financial advisor. To be certain, families' lives can be greatly improved with the right advice and made more comfortable. But there is another reason to get professional financial help, and that is to be defensive. The wonderful advancements in health care, life expectancy, and technology will have a financial effect that will be devastating for some. Consider: in this lifetime, entire industries will be disintermediated, while at the same time we all will live longer. This leaves those affected in a financial quandary...and an emotional one, at that. Having the foresight to deal with seismic shifts, and deal with them calmly, is simply not a reasonable expectation. In this situation, the risks of making a significant financial mistake can be significant.

Throughout this book, you will read about various types of people I have interviewed. There are consumers, investors, financial advisors, and senior leaders of firms that support advisors. Their stories are all terrific, and you will likely learn something from each one. It is important to note that many of the investor interviews are with people whom I was only recently introduced to by others. The randomness of how I came to them is informative, as they all have the common theme of not knowing how advisors could have improved their lives.

I am not an advisor, so outside of more copies of this book being sold, I do not benefit if more people get a financial advisor. If the percentage of advised families does not change, all the current financial advisors will be just fine. In fact, there is a shortage of advisors, so as older advisors retire, younger advisors will benefit even more. The reason I wrote this book is that I have a great interest in seeing more families improve their financial well-being.

To be clear, I am aware the financial advice industry is not a perfect one; simply put, there are bad actors in the industry. However, spending seven years in regulatory compliance gave me a unique insight in how to reduce the chances of encountering the wrong type. I also have the valuable experience of building database companies where I saw how many advisors had problematic histories, though thankfully, the bad actor rate is low. Most importantly, I have worked very closely with advisors for years, witnessed their investments first-hand on behalf of clients, and spent time with advisors watching them collaborate in furtherance of their clients. In this book, I will show you how to reduce your risk of encountering the wrong advisor and how to recognize the best ones.

My hope is that after reading this book, people will feel more comfortable reaching out and engaging with advisors, or at least be less wary of doing so. My long-term goal is for consumers and investors to change the way they feel about financial advisors and see them more like medical doctors or attorneys—as professionals who are needed for an optimal life. There is a perfect financial advisor out there for you, regardless of your income or asset level, and armed with the information in this book, you will be prepared.

WHY WE ALL NEED FINANCIAL ADVISORS

In today's complex world, most people who are building careers need professional help to organize their finances. The reason: Maneuvering the personal finance world is complex because there are myriad savings and investment options. Rather than risk making bad financial decisions, we can hire financial advisors who will fashion a financial strategy that meets the essential parameters of our lifestyles. The result: A strong personal balance sheet and peace of mind—an idyllic state that hardworking Americans deserve. Leading a stress-free life in a frenetic world moving at warp speed has ascended to a moral imperative.

Events of the recent past have proven that millions of Americans have paid a hefty price for shoddy financial guidance. When you consider the cost to low-income families with no life insurance, middle-income families who unwisely chase that heavily touted hot stock, and multimillionaires swindled by that so-called friend at their country club, the cost to society spirals into the trillions. The upsetting fact is that these often-crippling costs are avoidable.

When hardworking Americans are taken to the cleaners by glib, fast-talking con artists who pretend to be financial professionals, they're understandably enraged. Once trusting and open-minded, they're suspicious and wary of all financial professionals. At this point, reason goes out the window. There is great truth to the expression "once bitten, twice shy." Consensus thinking goes like this: If one financial advisor is a crook, they must all be crooks. It's illogical, flawed reasoning, but understandable.

A headline-grabbing example is Bernie Madoff, now serving 150 years in a federal prison for defrauding investors of sixty-four billion dollars in 2009. His victims numbered in the thousands. Many were left stripped of their equity earmarked for retirement. Some of Madoff's victims were able to recoup part of their losses, but most had no choice but to face down an inescapable reality. Rather than enjoying their retirement years, many had to downsize and go back to work—not to the well-paid professions they once excelled at, but to low-paying jobs such as stocking supermarket shelves or selling consumer electronics in big-box chains. Meanwhile, Madoff, a bona fide sociopath without regret, sits in a prison cell enjoying three square meals a day. While he has had some skirmishes with hostile prisoners, the unfathomable reality is that he is a celebrity prisoner and treated as such by fellow prisoners and guards alike.

Unfortunately, naïve clients pay a hefty price for their bad decisions and, often, their sheer laziness. If they had invested time in carefully vetting the charlatan investment advisor, they wouldn't have joined the growing army of victims bilked of their savings.

PRO ATHLETES NEED SUPERSTAR COACHES, WRITERS NEED BRILLIANT EDITORS...

College and pro athletes have coaches. Great coaches take promising athletes and turn them into extraordinary performers who can compete with the best. The same is true for writers. Practically everything we read, outside of self-published works, have editors perfecting the content. Why? Because even superstar writers like Ernest Hemingway and John Steinbeck had editors to challenge, push, and make their work better.

For important endeavors, having a leader, coach, guru, or whatever you want to call him or her, is vital in maximizing that activity. The average person, no matter how savvy, is not capable of acting completely as his own financial advisor without some kind of direction. Financial advice is not static and finite; in fact, it's fluid, constantly changing with the times and erratic, unpredictable economies. Rules and regulations, governing taxes, estates, and investments, are frequently updated to reflect economic and political changes. Running parallel to these changes are changes in our lifestyles and careers. As we trek along life's uncertain highway, we need financial advice that adapts to the changes taking place around us.

It's the smart person in touch with and on top of a constantly changing world who realizes the need for expert advice from a trained and experienced financial advisor. As our situation changes, it's often not one advisor who provides advice, but several, each one providing a service that's right at certain moments in time. In short, Americans need and deserve financial advisors to help them maximize their finances, so they can fully enjoy the fruits of their hard work. To continue the metaphor above, pro golfer Tiger Woods is a good example of this. He outgrew his first coach (his father) and went on to hire professional coaches.

DISPASSIONATE THIRD PARTY, IDEAL FOR SMART DECISIONS

Imagine this scenario: How would we feel with no money worries? That means no money arguments with our spouses about buying *that* expensive sofa, or trying to explain to her or him that it wouldn't be prudent to spend money to build a swimming pool. Or having to tell our kids that we can't afford to pay for a private college because it's too expensive, and that they have no choice but to apply for considerably less expensive state schools.

Or imagine bypassing soul-searching conversations with ourselves about why it's fiscally imprudent to buy a new luxury car with all the bells and whistles— even though we want those sexy new wheels.

Every day, such arguments and discussions over money take place all over America. They're part of our culture. But they and the angst that goes with them can be dramatically reduced to no longer dominate our lives. I'd be lying to you if I said it's possible to eliminate all our money problems. But they can be significantly reduced by getting help and guidance from experienced financial advisors. Just knowing that they are there and can offer positive advice significantly reduces our anxiety over money issues.

Practically every hardworking American dreams about having all his financial problems lifted from his shoulders. What better evidence than Americans' obsession with the lottery? Even though the chances of winning the lottery are miniscule, the compelling, adrenaline-charged fantasy that they *could* win, however remote, propels many to play.

AMERICANS SPEND FAR MORE THAN THEY SHOULD

Americans in the forty-three states where lotteries are legal annually spend about eighty billion dollars on lotto games, according to the North American Association of State and Provincial Lotteries. That breaks down to more than 230 dollars for every man, woman, and child in those states—or three hundred dollars for each adult. That's more than Americans in all fifty states spend on sports tickets, books, video games, movie tickets, and recorded music sales.

Practically speaking, however, it makes sense to do everything within our means to reduce our financial worries and get our financial act in order. Angst reduction alone is a wonderful benefit of having a professional we can call upon when stressed about money. Aside from providing expert advice, advisors can defuse our irrational, emotional involvement with money.

Human beings get overly involved in their decisions about money, making it very difficult to divorce ourselves from them. Many studies have found that investors fall in love with the stocks they buy. An irrational, emotional involvement with their purchases makes it difficult to sell them at the right time.

In 1987, when I was a rookie broker at Shearson Lehman Hutton in New York City during the famous stock market crash, I witnessed firsthand clients begging their brokers to sell their stocks without even knowing their individual prices. Sell orders were coming in so quickly that market technology could hardly keep up with them.

This was a textbook example of panic. Unable to see beyond the emotionally charged moment, investors threw reason and rational thinking to the wind and made a lot of bad decisions they later regretted. You can imagine how thousands of investors who panicked during that historic period must have felt a year later when the market hit new heights and kept on going.

How many times have we bought stocks near their highs and then sold low? Likely during every market bust. But then we complain about how lousy the market is. How many times have our stocks risen, yet we kept thinking they will continue to climb, and fail to take profits at the right moment? The stocks suddenly plummet, and we're forced to wait a couple of years until they come back. An advisor could have prevented those irrational moves and given us the perspective we needed.

Financial advisors can be likened to shrinks, rabbis, priests, or pastors, because they take the stress and tension out of financial planning. We don't have to endure angst about paying tuition for our offspring's first year of college or obsess about the poor performance of our 401(k) plans. Instead of expending needless energy worrying about these issues, we can dump them in our advisors' lap. They're the objective voice of reason that can unemotionally and objectively evaluate problems, providing sound and practical solutions.

WEALTH MANAGEMENT CAN BE LEARNED ON THE WEEKEND, RIGHT?

Wrong. Can just anyone do *our* jobs? Of course not. Then how can we think we're capable of doing a financial advisor's job? I'm talking about professionals who spend eight-plus hours a day on the job and several years studying to be experts in their field.

I relish clients who take nothing for granted and question everything they read, don't hesitate to question everything advisors do, and don't blindly accept everything advisors recommend because they are experts. Putting aside the training, expertise, and experience, not even advisors are infallible. They're human beings who make mistakes—infrequently, we hope. I love skeptical, knowledgeable clients, because they take a proactive approach and keep advisors razor sharp. If they disagree, or they don't understand the recommendations, they call to ask for explanations. Top advisors welcome interactive relationships with their clients. Not only do they trigger confidence in the decisions, but they also keep the advisor super vigilant. The result is productive, open, relaxed client-advisor relationships.

I urge clients to read respected financial magazines like *Money*, *Fortune*, and *Kiplinger's*. They publish timely articles on all aspects of personal financial management, ranging from investing in stocks and bonds to the intricacies of investing in covered call options.

Unquestionably, it's well worth the effort. I strongly suggest that clients stay on top of the stock market and read as much as they can about personal finance issues. The more they read, the better they understand the issues affecting their financial lives. Knowledge prompts smart questions, because once clients understand and appreciate what advisors do, they realize they need the services provided. I can't resist quoting the late New York City clothing entrepreneur Sy Syms' advertising slogan: "*An educated consumer* is our best customer."

From the client's perspective, it's reassuring to know that the advisor community is highly regulated. They are governed by state, federal, and self-regulated organizations, and are required to meet stringent requirements.

It's also important to know that most advisors invest countless hours staying on top of their field. They routinely network with other financial advisors and attend conferences, seminars, and lectures so that they are up to date on innovations and other changes in their field. Being totally immersed in their field, sometimes up to twelve to fourteen hours a day, often six days a week, gives them the perspective and knowledge to offer their clients state-of-the-art advice.

REVELATION: MOST PEOPLE DO NOT FIND WEALTH MANAGEMENT EXCITING

When we think about the important role our finances play in our lives, it is fascinating that most people do not find wealth management interesting. We all understand the importance of making smart financial decisions, considering our lifestyles, spending, savings, investments, retirement, vacations, and college education, as well as the peace of mind that comes from astute financial planning; however, given our understanding of its import, it is fascinating from a human behavior perspective how disconnected we become when it comes to taking action.

It's about bettering and improving our lives and eliminating continual anxiety over money. Smart wealth management, under the tutelage of an experienced financial advisor, is the vehicle leading to a worry-free lifestyle, and over time, increased wealth as a result of constructively tweaking spending habits and making smart investment decisions.

In light of such life-altering investments, the results of good wealth management does indeed fire our adrenaline, be it that dream home, car, or vacation. However, it is not hard to understand why many people think it's a boring subject, because they've taken on the tedious project of managing their finances themselves without the help of financial advisors. Why the mere prospect of reading technical documents, such as 401(k) statements, can drive laypeople to drink. Poring over incomprehensible fine print is an agonizing process requiring the patience of Job.

It's human nature to avoid what doesn't interest us. But consider the price we pay by ignoring the critical issue of wealth management. I repeatedly urge consumers to see this issue in a new light. If we have financial advisors taking the tedium out of managing our finances, acting as intermediaries, simply explaining the technical jargon, translating the corporate- and government-speak, we can concentrate on enjoying the improvement in our personal and family balance sheets.

Understand that people can't be masters of all trades. It's impossible. That's why we have myriad specialists we can avail ourselves of to make our lives better. Financial advisors are among them. They are part of our arsenal of specialists who have dedicated their careers to improving our lives—giving us peace of mind in the bargain. Doesn't it feel great just to ponder the prospect of going to sleep without a financial worry in the world?

WE DON'T KNOW WHAT WE DON'T KNOW

Cash is tangible because we can touch it, and it can bring immediate gratification. But intangibles, by their very nature, are harder to appreciate. Financial advice is one of the hardest intangibles to appreciate. Hence, we don't know we are missing something or have made a mistake. If lucky, we learn before we make mistakes. If unlucky, we learn too late. Having an advisor to guide us gives us the benefit of learning what we don't know. They say "ignorance is bliss," and sometimes that is indeed true. However, not knowing how to avoid financial calamity is not blissful. It's like playing financial Russian roulette.

In retrospect, one unforgettable example is Bernie Madoff's magnet-like attraction to investors, especially wealthy ones. This charismatic con man didn't have to hard-sell potential clients. They willingly sought him out and couldn't wait to turn their money over to him. At the height of his fame, he had a reputation for turning away investors who didn't meet his wealth parameters.

Well-heeled investors thought it a badge of honor to have the now infamous Bernie Madoff manage their money. At the time, the dozens of potential clients Madoff turned away didn't realize how lucky they were. Ironically, in light of all the lives he destroyed, the rejected clients have the last laugh.

Madoff was a scoundrel of Olympian proportions who broke all the rules. For example, he didn't use an independent bank to hold his clients' money, which is a common industry practice. (More on the SEC's failure to catch Madoff later.)

The uber-wealthy are not the only ones suckered by sociopathic Ponzi schemers. One year after Madoff was handcuffed and taken to his new home (the Butner Federal Correctional Institution in North Carolina, where he will spend the rest of his days), Long Island-based Nicholas Cosmo—dubbed the "Mini Madoff"—was caught stealing more than three hundred million dollars. Cosmo created fake investments and sold them to middle-income investors. The red flag that attracted the authorities' attention was Cosmo's promised 30 percent return on investments. Any advisor worth his salt would have stopped clients in their tracks from giving Cosmo money to invest for them. Unfortunately, most middle-income investors don't have financial advisors looking over their shoulders. Sadly, thousands of naïve investors were robbed because they didn't know what questions to ask.

YOU CANNOT PLAY EVERY POSITION ON THE FIELD

When most people, including the media, think of financial advisors, they think of them in the singular—one person acting as their financial guru. Over the past twenty years, however, the team concept has become the state-of-the-art method for providing financial advice. This is because administering financial advice has become much more sophisticated, thanks to the creation of high-tech solutions that solve more problems. For example, eldercare advice didn't exist twenty years ago, nor did exchange traded funds (ETFs), or same-sex financial planning. Because the industry is solving more problems, no one advisor can be an expert in all things financial. Hence, the concept of advisors either formally or informally teaming up with complimentary experts. To use a sports analogy, one athlete cannot be quarterback, running back, and kick returner, just as one financial advisor cannot be an expert in all financial services. In short, we need an advisor to be a gateway to the other experts we may need throughout our lives.

RECOURSE WITH ADVISORS, NONE ALONE

While we cannot abdicate our financial lives to our financial advisors, if something goes wrong and mistakes are made, we are entitled to recoup losses. And when clients screw up by failing to be proactive, they risk paying a hefty price— deservedly so. Practically speaking, when we outsource wealth management to a professional, he or she works for us. We can demand service, explanations, and— most important—performance.

WE NEED TO SAVE THE BILLIONAIRES

There is a ripple effect when a billionaire gets taken in by a fraud. For most incredibly well-off people, they are smart enough not to put all their money with any one particular investment. There were a few ultra-high net worth investors that put a lot with Madoff, Sanford and others, and indeed the ripple effect closed down charities, caused workers to be fired, and produced other horrible results. If someone worth three billion dollars loses one hundred fifty million dollars to a fraudster, odds are life goes just fine for that family.

However, the real reason we all want fewer billionaires to be taken in by frauds is the public relations effect. When someone rich is a victim, it becomes news, and it becomes outsized news at that. It stays in the news cycle longer than it should, and regular people from middle class families to higher-net worth people think if it that rich guy got taken to the cleaners, what hope do I have?

TWO KINDS OF CHANGE MANDATE THE USE OF AN ADVISOR

If the world were a static place with rules and situations that remain the same, life would be easier. But this is not the case. First, the personal finance world changes at a pace that makes it hard for even professional advisors to keep up. Second, consumers' lives are constantly changing. They marry, change jobs, travel, have children, get sick, and the list goes on.

When these two types of change are combined, it's an overwhelming process to try to maximize our personal financial situation alone. Hence, the need for financial advisors—with professional expertise, experience, emotional distance, and objectivity—to take this burden off our hands.

CHAPTER 2

WHO SAID YOU HAVE TO BE RICH TO HIRE A FINANCIAL ADVISOR?

The general public has only a vague idea of why financial advisors are important and the impact they have on our lives. They're doing far more than providing financial advice. They're customizing advice to meet their clients' unique financial goals and objectives.

Customized advice leads to smart investments, increased savings, and often a marked jump in disposable income, which translate to a better and stress-free lifestyle. While most consumers understand the importance of savings and smart investing—albeit often too late—they need help with organizing their finances.

A recent Gallup Poll found that two-thirds of Americans prefer saving to spending, and most need help fashioning a savings strategy that positively affects their lifestyles. But that hasn't always been the case. Until fairly recently, most Americans were lax about financial planning, especially the baby boomer generation (1946–64). The following alarming statistics drive this point home:

1. More than 40 percent of Americans can't afford to retire, according to a report by the American Institute of Certified Public Accountants.

2. Four of ten Americans have retirement savings of less than ten thousand dollars, and three out of ten Americans have retirement savings of less than one thousand dollars.

3. In recent years, Americans spent more than they earned.

4. Social Security provides 73 percent of the typical retiree's income, compared with 17 percent from pensions, and 10 percent from savings and other sources.

5. Without Social Security, more than 40 percent of Americans ages sixty-five and older would live in poverty.

6. Boomers' retirement accounts are grossly underfunded, according to a survey conducted by the Insured Retirement Institute (IRI). The IRI survey found that only 19 percent of boomers have two hundred fifty thousand dollars or more saved for retirement, while four in ten have nothing saved.

EVERYONE CAN BENEFIT FROM AN ADVISOR

Contrary to popular opinion, everyone—regardless of savings, income or investments—can benefit from a financial advisor's services. That's because today's advisors offer a robust list of services, from cash-flow planning and reducing taxes, to paying for college, to investing in specialized securities for enhanced returns.

There are more than two million financial and insurance advisors in the United States. Many are generalists, while others offer specialized advice based upon clients' needs and goals.

More important than whether we're poor or wealthy, or how good we think our investing or planning skills are, there is a local advisor who can improve our lives—not just our financial lives, but our entire lives. When we think about the totality of our lives, which encompasses our lifestyles, our family's health and welfare, and our disposable income, our finances dictate how we live. Our finances create both opportunities and limitations. They dictate the type of neighborhoods we live in, the type of friendships we cultivate, the schools our children attend, and the type of restaurants we frequent. Our finances define our social status, and—most important—how we feel about ourselves.

Most people don't realize that financial advisors can level the playing field for everyone, especially the millions struggling to make ends meet.

BROAD SPECTRUM OF SERVICES AND DIVERSE CLIENTELE

Advisors offer a smorgasbord of services that cater to clients in all income categories. The following four groups are excellent examples.

1. Garrett Planning Network

The Garrett Planning Network is a nationwide group of financial planners who offer reasonably priced hourly financial advice geared for the average household, with no asset minimums. Hundreds of advisors are in the network. The advisory community has lauded the network for its unique platform, which helps clients and also trains advisors to provide advice that anyone can take advantage of. While the Garrett Planning Network is well-known and highly respected in the industry and has received a significant amount of positive press, after more than fifteen years, it still doesn't have the name recognition that it deserves among consumers. That means thousands of families are not getting the help they need.

The Garrett Network is just one example of advisors who can be hired on a simple hourly basis, without minimums or significant time commitments.

Sheryl Garrett has been enabling advisors to provide financial planning for middle America clients for over eighteen years. Through her Garrett Planning Network, Sheryl estimates that between ten thousand and twenty-five thousand people per year have benefitted from her group's fee-only hourly financial planning services. Over 230 advisors are in her network, which provides a turnkey solution to teach planners on how to serve the middle market.

Sheryl has been in the financial industry for thirty-one years. At the age of twenty-four, she started at IDS, the predecessor firm to Ameriprise. From there she worked at a traditional financial planning practice—that catered to affluent families—but she had a yearning for serving middle income families and decided to leave and start her own planning practice in 1998. After only two years, Sheryl had so many clients and so many referrals from other planners for her unique brand of no asset minimum and hourly planning services that she was at her personal capacity. With the support and encouragement of others in the industry she started the Garrett Planning Network.

Through her years of experience, Sheryl has learned many things through serving middle market clients. She also has learned much from her network of over two hundred advisors, as they as a group heavily share knowledge across her network. For example, many times we get second opinions from another doctor when we hear a diagnosis; why not apply the same idea to financial advice? Sheryl shared that sometimes she meets investors who are under the false belief that the advice they have been getting is free and did not understand that indeed they were paying a fee, but it was through the investments recommended.

She firmly believes that everyone should at least have access to an advisor at the right time, because there are consumers and/or investors that like to manage some of their own financial affairs, but want to reach out with situations they are uncomfortable with. For example, if you are not sure if the cost of your retirement account is appropriate or if you are thinking perhaps you could minimize taxes in your holdings, getting a planner to offer an opinion might make sense.

When searching for an advisor, Sheryl offers that you should get everything in writing before selecting an advisor, including the all-in costs of the advice so you are clear. It's vitally important to have a very good relationship with any potential advisor. Finally, the investor-advisor personal relationship is critically important. If you are not communicating with each other well, the best advice in the world is not helpful if the advice is not followed.

2. XY Planning Network

The XY Planning Network is a nationwide planning network that caters to the Generations X and Y demographic. For a reasonable retainer fee, the network offers monthly virtual advice. This technology-enabled service provides monthly budgeting and financial planning advice, which is highly desired by younger investors. I share much more about XY in my interview with their co-founder in the chapter on Millennials.

3. Foundation for Financial Planning

The Foundation for Financial Planning is a national nonprofit organization that offers free financial planning advice to those in need. The foundation supports dozens of local nonprofits that help disaster victims, returning military personnel, and others. Over the past year alone, tens of thousands of free financial planning hours were donated to those in need. The last chapter of this book cover pro-bono planning and advice, and also my interview with the Foundation's CEO.

4. Financial Planning Association of New York

This is one of many groups around the country affiliated with the Financial Planning Association. The FPANY group provides free advice to more than twenty New York City organizations, including departments that serve battered women, the indigent, and single parents. Also, in chapter 20 I share an interview with one of the volunteer planners, as well as details on other chapters that have a pro bono effort.

PUBLIC HAS WRONG IDEA ABOUT FINANCIAL ADVICE

Sadly, most Americans know little or nothing about financial advisors. The result is that more than half of all American households have never taken advantage of financial advisors' services. Typically, it's because of three biases:

1. People think their finances are not complicated enough to warrant the services of an advisor.

2. They don't know how an advisor can better their lives by changing and improving their finances.

3. They don't think they can afford an advisor.

These three biases are incorrect.

Equally important, most people don't know how to find an advisor who can best serve them.

THE COST OF FINANCIAL ADVICE

Most people would be surprised, even stunned, to learn that the cost of advice can almost be literally whatever our budgets allow. Someone at the poverty level, for example, can get free financial advice.

ADVISORS SERVE A DIVERSE POPULATION

Now that I've debunked the myth that advisors serve only the well-heeled, consider that there are advisors who cater to recent grads, thirty-somethings, mid-career builders, and many others. Some firms do only hourly planning and neither sells anything nor charge based on our assets. Other firms charge an annual retainer fee, and still others charge based on our total asset value. And some firms charge a commission based on the sales of products we need. The fees can be as low as two hundred dollars for a consultation all the way up to many thousands per year.

These examples illustrate that the highly regulated financial advisory community is working not only to improve its image, but also to expand its services, so it caters to people in all income brackets.

The important message is that the financial advisory niche has grown and changed enormously. Thirty years ago, individual investors only had two payment options: commissions or a percent of a portfolio's value. Today, we have a raft of options to choose from.

FINANCIAL ADVICE DOESN'T ALWAYS CENTER ON INVESTING

Clients are surprised to learn that the most impactful advice often doesn't center on investing. Still, making the right asset allocation, and avoiding highly speculative or overly conservative stocks or fund selections is critically important. However, for many people, far more impactful financial advice decisions can improve our lives.

Consider this true story. A forty-five-year-old who cancelled a life insurance policy to save 140 dollars per month wound up paying more than ten thousand dollars per year. Several years after canceling his policy, he developed a non-life-threatening cancer. Canceling the policy was a big mistake. An advisor would have urged him not to cancel his policy.

In other cases, advisors have vetted investment deals or scams and prevented clients from losing significant amounts of money.

Today's advisors are trained to guide clients on practically anything to do with money or affected by money. The following sections are a brief sampling of the benefits and services that advisors provide to individuals and families.

RETIREMENT PREPARATION

Retirement planning is the best-known aspect of wealth management. Every day, TV commercials are aired by advisors on ways to retire. And the government has substantive programs to help people retire. However, as any financial advisor will tell you, retirement planning and saving is not as simple as putting away a certain amount of money in an index fund and forgetting about it. Many important decisions are to be made, such as the appropriate amount to save. With hundreds of index funds to choose from, which ones yield the best results? And what type of account—IRA, 401(k), Roth IRA—best meets our needs?

Employers also factor into our decision. What kind of plans do they offer? If married, have you compared plans with your spouse? What do you estimate your expenses will be when you retire? What quality of life will meet your needs? When the layers are peeled back, the depth of the issue is astounding.

Another way to appreciate and understand the need for an advisor to guide you through the retirement-planning maze is to look at the advisor trade publications. Many insightful articles are written by advisors who are experts on the subject. It's impressive to see how well-informed they are and how impressive their qualifications.

POST-RETIREMENT NEEDS

Once you are retired, life is very different for reasons that are not obvious. For openers, how much of your retirement money is safe to spend each year? Is it the 4 percent many experts write about or is it a different number? Inflation and cost of living affect this number. The last thing you want to do is outlive your money. However, you also want to enjoy your retirement, if in fact you can afford to retire. How do Social Security rules affect your retirement? I doubt that you want to grope through the highly technical two-hundred-plus-page books written about Social Security and how to take advantage of all the current rules. Advisors take this depressing chore off our hands.

INSURANCE NEEDS

Insurance is one of the hardest wealth topics to deal with because it's not only complicated, it's also emotional—far more so than any other aspect of wealth management. We don't like to talk, or even think, about our death. And we don't like thinking about getting ill, yet both are inevitable. And if we don't plan for these eventualities, our lives and those of our loved ones may be devastated. Being properly insured for the unexpected is more important than beating the S&P. An insurance advisor will explain what is needed given our lifestyles and future plans.

INVESTING NEEDS

Most, but not all, advisors provide guidance on which securities offer the best short- and long-term returns. When it comes to investing, there are many decisions to be made and thousands of securities from which to choose. Advisors can choose a group of mutual funds, or select individual stocks and bonds, or both. They can also set up what is called a Separate Account, which is managed by other advisors who only manage money.

There are thousands of Separate Account providers. Financial advisors can replace Separate Account providers much like selecting and replacing funds, stocks, or alternative investments, such as hedge funds, private equity, venture capital investments, and options, normally bought and sold by wealthy investors who can afford the risk these investments carry. Generalist advisors provide advice on all the above, and others specialize in providing one service, such as the following.

CASH-FLOW NEEDS

Advisors who offer financial-planning services or wealth management services analyze our cash flow. By evaluating what we spend our money on every month, they can suggest areas for savings. Most important, they educate their clients on what our money can do for us if saved or invested. For many Americans, this service is critical, because as a consumer culture, the pressure to spend for immediate gratification is irresistible. For many, the urge to spend money on things we want but don't need lies somewhere between obsession and addiction. An advisor can objectively advise us about where we're spending needlessly and what it is costing us.

Helping People with Small or No Investment Portfolios

If we have no stocks, bonds, or mutual funds, or if we have a tiny retirement fund, we're likely to think a financial advisor's services are unaffordable. But just the opposite is true. We need an advisor more than someone with a one-million-dollar portfolio. The reason is that every decision we make about spending, savings, education, careers, insurance, food, and so on, means more to us than to someone with an established nest egg. Financial planning is the service we need. A financial plan to achieve our goals looks at all these issues. Financial planners ask us questions we never thought of. Their candid advice helps us achieve those goals.

THOSE WITH SIGNIFICANT PORTFOLIOS

Many people with large portfolios know that plenty of financial advisors would love to manage their accounts. But they question whether they need them, which is a mistake. Advisors can provide services they're not aware of. For example, complex tax issues need to be understood if one is to maximize one's portfolios. Advisors provide advice on all aspects of investing, such as active versus passive investing, and the right mix of stocks and bonds, taking into consideration interest rates and retirement goals.

THOSE WITH LOW INCOMES

Either a flat-fee financial planner or free financial help from one of the nonprofits mentioned in this book makes the most sense. Low income earners could benefit from financial guidance about all things impacted by money, such as budgeting, insurance, and retirement planning.

THOSE WITH HIGH INCOMES

Because they have much to protect, quality insurance advice is essential. If you are single and a high earner, disability insurance should be a top priority in case you become ill. If married, both disability and life insurance are needed because you have dependents to protect. With high incomes come tax and budgeting complications to consider. High earners are constantly being pitched by brokers selling every conceivable investment opportunity under the sun. Advisors gate-keep these opportunities and vet them for their clients. Being highly successful in our careers does not automatically equate to being adept at investing. Very often, it's just the opposite, as many of Bernie Madoff's victims discovered.

BUSINESS OWNERS WHOSE PRIMARY ASSET IS THEIR BUSINESSES

Many business owners have all their wealth tied up in their businesses. Most of American wealth is created by small businesses.

Business owners have unique needs and challenges. Because they work sixty to eighty or more hours per week, they don't have the time to deal with personal finance issues. Decisions made at the business level concerning taxes, health benefits, family issues, and investing in the business for expansion, affect business owners and their families. Savvy business owners realize their limitations, especially when it comes to making critical decisions that affect both their businesses and their families. They hire advisors who specialize in working with small-business owners. Advisors help them with complicated issues concerning retirement, succession planning, and selling the business, for example—as well as divisive internal problems, such as hiring and firing relatives.

INHERITANCES, GIVING AND RECEIVING

Who wouldn't want to be left a hefty portfolio of blue chip stocks by a rich uncle? Or be in a position to leave the family farm after it was passed from one generation to the next for close to a century?

However, rarely do these events take place without enormous work and stress. If you are fortunate enough to be in this position, there is much to consider. Of course, minimizing taxes is a top priority. But practically managing money is an emotionally charged issue that often drives families apart and hurdles business owners into bankruptcy. Few people can handle sudden wealth. Fewer still can deal with the stresses and tensions of their families lining up for their wealth, or of creating fair mechanisms to divide an estate after death.

For example, one story I refer to centers around a woman who was one of many family members that inherited the family's blueberry farm in New England. The original owner happened to be an attorney who created a trust so that duties and responsibilities for managing the farm were clearly outlined for future generations. But the trust was set up with insufficient detail, failing to account for family members saddled with responsibilities that they did not want or were incapable of handling. A gift bestowed with good intentions turned out to be a mixed blessing.

So you see, everyone, regardless of income and assets, can benefit from an advisor. Just as we all would do well to have an annual medical checkup, we could benefit from an advisor to guide us on all things financial. It's a smart decision that can improve our lives and give us peace of mind in the bargain. It's a no-brainer decision because we have nothing to lose and everything to gain.

CHAPTER 3

WHO SAYS FINANCIAL ADVISORS DON'T CARE ABOUT MILLENNIALS?

Possibly the millennials—those born between 1982 and 1994—are jealous of all the attention baby boomers have been getting since January 1, 2011, when the oldest members of the baby boom generation turned sixty-five. On that day—and for every day for the next nineteen years—ten thousand baby boomers will reach age sixty-five.

Surveys show that millennials don't trust financial advisors. However, surveys can be damaging, especially if their conclusions are questionable. But most consumers believe survey results because they're easy to remember. And in a sound-bite society where content is king and most young people are short on patience and in a frenetic rush to succeed, many consumers opt not to read. Why bother when they can absorb bite-size, real-time content 24/7 on their iPhones? The average consumer hardly questions survey standards and methods, such as the number of people surveyed and whether they're a representative sample.

A survey conducted by research firm Corporate Insight found that that the investment industry is discriminating against millennials. Based on a survey of five hundred advisors, only 30 percent of financial advisors are actively looking for clients under age forty. It's widely (but incorrectly) believed that advisors prefer older clients because they have money, and thus are not interested in millennials. It's time to right the scales and bridge the millennial/financial advisor misinformation gap.

A report by research firm Accenture showed that the millennial generation is determined to leave a financial legacy for their children. Millennials also tend to be more financially conservative than baby boomers and Generation X.

According to the U.S. Census bureau, Millennials are the largest generational group in recent history at ninety-two million, larger than the boomers at seventy-seven million. They have less money to spend, according to the bureau of labor statistics, due to smaller incomes. They have twice the debt—in the form of student loan debt—of those from ten years ago, according to the Federal Reserve. As a result, commitments like marriage and home buying are being delayed. With the unique characteristics of this group, their need for financial advice is considerable, but needs to be differently formatted than previous generations. The supply of those serving Millennials is adapting to this new type of consumer/investor.

Millennials have a harder time with finding advisors because of the popular notion that they need a portfolio of securities to be managed, and therefore, simply do not look for an advisor. Many in this age group simply are not aware of the other services advisors offer, so they do not conduct a search for someone that can help.

ON A BETTER PATH

Angela Poupart, the daughter of missionaries, is thirty-one and grew up in the Midwest. Due to good parenting, Angela was unaware she came from a lower income household. Early on, she was taught the perspective that climbing the corporate ladder would grant her success, but that never appealed to her, and her overall quest wasn't centered around becoming a millionaire. She is a creative person who likes to understand the functionalities of the things around her, which led her to becoming more inquisitive about her finances and how they were being managed in her life.

She went to community college to save money, then transferred and graduated from Ohio State University with a degree in New Media and Communication Technology. She is fascinated with the topic of human computer interaction and understanding how people interact with product interfaces. Upon graduating, she accumulated thirty thousand dollars in school debt, something she is not comfortable with as her parents taught her that debt can be very problematic. Angela wants to accomplish several things in her personal finance journey. She wants to invest for retirement, but also fund her passions. She feels that there is a narrative that investing is only for retirement, but not for being a tool to pursue your dreams, which for her may include starting a business one day. Her frustrations stem from not knowing where to start looking for the right resources to help her and feeling unsure of which steps to take.

Angela went to someone who has been in the financial services industry for over thirty years and asked this person what she should do. The reply? "Until you have twenty-five thousand dollars to invest, there is not much you can do." This same person also suggested reading the *Wall Street Journal* every day. She did read the *WSJ* for a while, but was not able to connect to it, and found it was not answering her questions. Angela told me this was not the first time someone gave her advice that was not helpful. This advice was pretty bad for her; in fact, this is simply not correct for anyone in her situation.

During our interview, I told her there were thousands of advisors who catered specifically to Gen X and Y consumers. I followed up by telling her about the XY Planning Network, a company that teaches advisors how to set up a financial planning practice to cater to this demographic and has a directory of members to select from. There are over six hundred advisors that belong to this network. Angela can get an affordable financial planner who will tell her all the things she should be thinking about financially. Angela is among the many who do not know what they don't know. If you're in this situation, getting a financial planner is the best thing you can do for yourself.

Angela has since moved to New York, paid down a good amount of her debt, and is actively evaluating different planners. Angela had a great view on why she plans to get a financial planner. "We all put at least forty hours of work into our job and spend an incredible amount of effort into doing our job well. The output of that work is money, yet so many people don't put any effort into what to do with the money afterwards. The effort should be continuous throughout the whole cycle, but it's not. It makes no sense."

A LONG-TERM RELATIONSHIP

Barry (not his real name) is single, thirty-seven, and a cyber security expert who has an MBA. Barry describes himself as a methodical person who does not get rattled easily. Barry has had the same advisor since right after graduating college, and in fact he uses the advisor his parents have been using. Mark (not his real name) has been working with Barry's parents for many years, coming to the house to discuss various issues, so Barry has known him for a long time. Mark started his career as an insurance agent, then later got his series 7 license and now only gives investment advice and securities brokerage services, no longer selling insurance. When Barry was about to graduate from college, Mark invited him to his office to give him tips on his résumé and job hunting. Barry was very appreciative, and found it refreshing that Mark took an interest in Barry's career and future.

In Barry's first job, he participated in his employer's 401(k), then started getting guidance from Mark. Later, he opened an IRA and a Roth IRA with Mark and contributed as much as he could each year. During the 2008 recession, Mark called Barry very frequently to see how Barry was doing, as so many people were rattled and making emotional decisions. Barry had to tell Mark to call less often; he was fine, and understood markets go down. He was confident in his investments.

Over the years, Barry has met with other advisors, but none have given him the comfort level Mark has. Mark understands what level of detail and information Barry needs, is always prepared, and knows when to persist on a certain topic and when not to. Barry's primary goal is to fund retirement, and possibly get out of the corporate life and start his own business in the future, in order to control his own earnings destiny. Because he started early and stayed the course, he is on pace—and in fact, ahead—of most of his peers.

AN ENTIRE ORGANIZATION FOR MILLENNIALS

Michael Kitces is the co-founder of XY Planning Network, an organization with over six hundred advisor-members who provide financial planning services to Generation X and Y consumers. Michael has been in the industry eighteen years and is very well known in the financial advice and financial planning communities. He is also a partner and Director of Wealth Management of Pinnacle Advisory Group, as well as founder of his Kitces.com and Nerd's Eye Blog, and finally, co-founder of AdvicePay—an application that makes it easier for advisors to charge monthly retainer or other financial planning fees while safely complying with SEC rules. He holds two master's degrees and many designations, including the CFP, CLU, and ChFC.

XY Planning Network (XYPN) was founded in 2014 in response to an observation by Michael and co-founder Alan Moore that there was not enough focus on helping consumers who needed and wanted financial advice, but who had not yet accumulated an investment portfolio to give an advisor to manage in exchange for that advice. Alan had in fact already been working with clients in their twenties and thirties when he and Michael decided to create a business around the notion that there are many younger consumers who need advice that is unrelated to managing an investment portfolio. XYPN is an organization that helps advisors set up and maintain a planning business for younger consumers that is fee-only and charges a reasonable monthly fee for financial planning advice. The network has many support programs for the advisor members, including bundled technology to run a fee-for-service planning firm, membership in a trade association, discounts on additional software licensing, and an advisor support system through access to a community of like-minded advisors. It is rapidly growing.

For a young consumer, selecting an advisor listed on the XY Planning Network website will provide access to a licensed CFP professional to answer myriad questions such as how to budget, how to manage cash flow, how to take advantage of employment benefits, how to save for a house down payment, and more. During my interview with Michael, he made the statement that many people refer to their attorney for legal advice and refer to their CPA for tax advice, so why not refer to a retained planner for anything and everything relating to money and wealth?

It is not difficult to think of topics to discuss with your personal financial planner as a younger person. Do I need life insurance? What are the best practices if I get married and need to merge household finances with my spouse? How do I deal with my student debt? Consumers should expect to pay between seventy and two hundred dollars per month to have an XYPN planner on retainer. During our discussion, Michael had a unique way of putting this recurring expense into perspective. "Have you made money mistakes in your life that amount to two percent or more of your annual income? For most people, the answer is yes. Therefore, paying between one to two percent of your annual income for a licensed CFP professional to rely upon to prevent you from making those mistakes going forward with the other 98 percent of your income is an excellent investment."

MILLENNIAL ADVISORS MAKE THEMSELVES KNOWN

The good news for investors in the Gen Y and Gen X age brackets is that advisors of that age are very comfortable making themselves known on social media platforms like Facebook, LinkedIn, Twitter, and others. They speak publicly with frequency, they write and blog, they are very social, and readily share their marketing best practices with others. There are even conferences about financial topics not unlike Comic-Con; one is called Fincon, where younger advisors speak, exhibit, and meet other financial gurus who are media savvy.

NOT YOUR FATHER'S FINANCIAL PLANNER

Sophia Bera is the founder of Gen Y Planning focusing on Millennials. Sophia is a CFP and understands what it's like to be a twenty-something figuring out how to prioritize all of life's financial decisions, from home buying to saving to paying off debt. As a virtual planner, she makes herself available at night and on the weekends to accommodate the busy lives of young professionals. She has appeared on TV, been interviewed, created a blog, and written an eBook titled *What You Should Have Learned About Money But Never Did*.

She makes the point that she is relatable to her clients, making them feel like they are speaking with an old friend via email, phone, or Skype. Sophia writes that she helps people use their money to create their ideal lives. She, like other advisors catering to a younger age bracket, charges a monthly retainer fee for planning services. A common point that has been made is that this younger generation pays many bills monthly, such as cable TV, rent, insurance, gym membership, and others; a financial planner or coach cost is acceptable as a monthly expense as well. A frequent public speaker, Sophia has addressed advisor audiences, consumer audiences, and employee audiences at firms like Google.

ADDRESSING A HUGE DISCONNECT

Workable Wealth, LLC is a financial planning firm catering to those in their twenties to forties. Mary Beth Storjohann is a CFP who has been making financial advice approachable and fun to professional and entrepreneurial women, young couples and families, and military families, for the last thirteen years. She makes the point that the Gen X and Gen Y market has not been served as well as it could be by the educational system nor the broader planning and financial sector. Mary Beth is part of a growing group of advisors that charge some manner of fee for planning services, normally a monthly retainer.

Mary Beth stands out, as she has been embraced by the media and has been interviewed by NBC, CNBC, *The Wall Street Journal*, *Forbes*, *Women's Health* and many other publications. As a military spouse, she has great affinity for those that serve and their families. As a young mother and entrepreneur, she has empathy for the financial and literal distractions that can make it difficult to master your financial life.

FROM GOOGLE TO PLANNER-ROBO

Chris Hutchins and Chris Doyle came to serve the financial advice needs of Millennials from different places, but arrived at a similar conclusion. Hutchins spent time at Google Ventures, and Doyle at Barclays working with mortgage backed securities. In 2015, they founded Grove in San Francisco to make financial advice and planning affordable to everyone.

Grove is different from the thousands of millennial-aged advisors serving millennials. They appear to be seeing a very large business for themselves in the future as they have a sizable staff and have created their own investment algorithm that goes hand in hand with staff CFPs. In fact, the process starts with a CFP-rendered financial plan. They are clearly targeting the competition with a low flat annual fee, plus a low asset under management fee for their own robo.

An impetus to start this business was an observation that Doyle made: even his sophisticated associates were unsure of how to address the various and complicated questions they had surrounding finances.

CHAPTER 4

TOP MYTHS ABOUT FINANCIAL ADVISORS

FINANCIAL ADVICE IS ALL ABOUT THE NUMBERS

Even the Numbers Are Not About the Numbers

Many people equate financial advice to some mathematical formula about determining what stocks, bonds, or mutual funds to invest in. Then they watch these investments and buy or sell based on how their prices rise and fall. This perception is a more accurate description of a mutual fund manager rather than a financial advisor who is managing an individual's money. When your client is sitting across the table from you and investing for a purpose, his future depends on you as the advisor doing your job.

So let's start with the "simple" scenario of a couple who is in their early fifties and need their portfolio managed so they can retire comfortably. These numbers turn very human, and very emotional, quite fast. To begin with, how long will this couple live? Imagine being the advisor and having to look at this couple and ask in one way or another, "So, Mr. and Mrs. Jones, when will you both die? I have to understand how long the money needs to last, after all, and your life expectancy needs to be estimated."

This question used to be pretty simple years ago, when life spans were rather fixed and did not change much. Most European countries as well as the U.S. kept age sixty-five as the standard retirement age. Today, however, modern medicine is changing so fast that big jumps in life span are likely. That needs to be factored in, because running out of money in retirement is one of the basic concepts every advisor and investor seeks to avoid; the subject makes for an emotionally charged interaction.

A related issue is the clients' health. Having these conversations with a client can be difficult, especially if the client is also facing serious medical issues. Financial advice becomes an emotional journey because the things people use their money for are human and affect their loved ones.

Let us discuss a not so simple question your advisor will ask you, assuming you have children: "Where do you want your kids to go to college?" Saving money now, possibly affecting your retirement savings, is going to factor into what kind of university your children go to. How much to save, what rate of return to assume the college savings account will generate, and what financial aid programs will exist in the future, are all questions that can generate an enormity of emotions. Moreover, most couples will have strife and anxiety and argue about saving for college, which adds to emotional angst.

Non-Numerical Advice Issues Are Emotional

The dreaded life insurance talk. For advisors, it's like the sex talk with their kids. Every parent dreads it and really hopes the high school guidance counselor or some documentary handles it before they have to. Advisors hate the life insurance talk because their clients resist it so much. Over 30 percent of American families do not have life insurance, according to LIMRAs 2016 Trends in Life Insurance Ownership study. Life insurance is sold—not purchased—because people hate talking about their death. It is wildly frustrating for an advisor to hammer into their client's head that the client needs life insurance because if they die early, their family is screwed and there is nothing worse than making that mistake. Even after the heartfelt plea, the charts, and the horror stories, 30 percent of clients refuse to follow through. If the advisor does their job correctly, emotional stress from the life insurance talk should make the consumer very uncomfortable until they actually sign the contract and make the first payment. Very emotional indeed, but one of the basics.

Your parents, if alive, are an emotional topic. Who will take care of them as they age? Do they have the money to have in-home care? Did they prepare for someone taking care of them? Are they going to move in with you? Are they going into a home? Will the guilt of any of these issues create incredible anxiety for you? Will this topic impact your marriage? Is the shoe on other foot, and are you the reader at an age where you do not want to burden your children? These can be very complex issues that involve law, taxes, investments, but more so, emotional issues of how to grapple with the decisions to make.

Family and the Numbers

Most financial planners will tell you to have between six and twelve months of living expenses saved in case of emergency. In order to accomplish that savings number, families need to make weekly and monthly decisions on what to not spend money on. That discussion is most often a highly charged issue between couples. If you have young children, that conversation becomes even more charged as demands from children become more acute and they approach their pre-teen years.

The bigger discussion is to even discuss money in the first place as a family. One of the main reasons for financial illiteracy is the fact that in the United States it is taboo to discuss money among family, friends, and children. Financial advisors have become part-time psychologists in order to get people to even begin the discussion to get to the numbers. There are entire books and courses written on the topic of financial illiteracy in the United States, and it is one of the reasons advisors' jobs have become even more needed, and more important. The very basics are unknown to so many, because of the stigma around money and what to do with it.

The numbers are only a small part of financial advisors do, and for some client families, the least important part of the job.

ADVISORS ARE SLICK AND RICH SALESPEOPLE

The Rich Fallacy

As shown in other chapters, most of the nation's financial advisors work for firms that are called "independent broker dealers," which are firms that do not have household name recognition. These advisors have clients that are generally small. Most advisors have two hundred or fewer clients, so when doing the math, these advisors simply do not become fabulously wealthy. The narrative that follows, of course, is supposedly advisors get rich at the expense of their clients. The numbers simply do not add up.

It is true that financial advisors in general make a decent living. Generally speaking, the larger the firm an advisor works for, the better they tend to do. The vast majority of financial advisors, however, do not become incredibly rich in short spans of time—as many hedge fund managers, who can make millions of dollars per year, do.

Research done by noted firms such as Cerulli, FRC, and others prove this. According to the 2016 *U.S. News and World Reports* Best Jobs Rankings, the median salary in dollars for financial advisors was 90,530, with the lowest at 41,150 and the highest at two hundred eight thousand. Bonuses could increase the figures.

Slick No More

The "slick factor" was much higher thirty years ago. The industry has changed dramatically, so much so that the industry trade publications and events now are offering training to help advisors be more social and gregarious. This is an effort to combat the last twenty-year trend of advisors being so technical about wealth management in their effort to show competency that many investors no longer understand what their advisors are trying to communicate due to the use of jargon and technical investment and planning terms.

Salespeople a Dying Breed

Thirty years ago, nearly all financial advisors sold securities to their clients. I, for a short time, was one of them. Stockbrokers existed for more than a hundred years prior to my short stint as one, but that was the industry then. Since the 1980s, the industry has changed dramatically, and there are far fewer pure salespeople left in the industry today.

Now, at FINRA firms, over 39 percent of all money invested on behalf of investors is in fee-based programs according to the 2017 Aite Group Study whereby the advisor is a representative of the FINRA firms' Registered Investment Adviser entity. Another consulting firm, Cerulli, has stated the percentage of client money being held in advisory accounts among traditional financial advisors had risen to 42 percent at the end of 2016 from 25 percent twelve years earlier. In plain English, many advisors today are suggesting clients invest in a program not dependent on making an individual security sale, rather managing a selection of investments in mutual funds, stocks, or other investment managers for an annual flat fee, generally 1–2 percent per year. This progression coupled with the growth of financial planning or wealth management has resulted in far fewer advisors who are making individual security sales.

FINANCIAL ADVISORS ARE IN THE POCKETS OF WALL STREET FIRMS

Approximately fifty thousand advisors work for the four largest brokerage firms that are considered "Wall Street." But there are close to eight hundred thousand financial advisors that compete with them at the other types of firms, and 1.2 million insurance professionals that are separate from both. Given these numbers, one can no longer say financial advisors are employed by Wall Street or heavily influenced by Wall Street.

Further proof is the reality that financial advisors come in all shapes and sizes, belong to dozens of competing trade organizations, and directly compete against each other. These independent financial advisors are not shy about broadcasting their perceived advantages over "Wall Street" firms and the advisors that work for them. Advisors are no longer this homogenous group.

Moreover, the financial products that most advisors recommend are now also less connected—or in some cases, completely unrelated to—Wall Street firms. Essentially, these days any advisor can obtain any type of investment for their client. The crowning example is Vanguard Funds, which is one of the world's largest mutual fund companies. Anyone can invest in a Vanguard fund, and in fact, many advisors at all types of competing firms have been putting their clients' money into Vanguard. Here is what people don't realize: Vanguard is owned by its shareholders—a mutually owned company. If you have one thousand dollars in a Vanguard fund, you technically are one of the owners of the company. Its stock is not traded on an exchange and its funds were not available through broker-dealers for most of its history. At over three trillion dollars in assets as of July 2017, Vanguard is almost twice the size of American Funds, which is the most beloved Broker-sold mutual fund. That is an amazing shift, and compelling proof that the power and influence shift has been dramatic.

"I'M SIMPLE, SO I DON'T NEED AN ADVISOR"

Are You Indeed "Simple"?

Very few people are truly introspective. It is very difficult—if not impossible—to have a truly objective view of yourself. If we could, there would be no reason for psychologists, psychologists, therapists, or clergy, for that matter. Financial issues are no different. Without perspective, one cannot even know if they are "simple."

Let's review the "simplest of simple" types of people. A young person, right out of college, and—to make this hypothetical person even "simpler"—they have no college debt. This person might say they do not need a financial advisor. No spouse, no kids, no real debt. However, there are many questions they need to answer if they want to lead a maximally fulfilled life. When do you want to retire? Do you want to have a family? Are your parents living, if so, will you be called upon to help them later in life? Do you want to own your own home? Do you want to go on at least one vacation per year? Do you have the best possible job right now and is it paying you what you need, or better yet, deserve?

For each of the above six questions, there are a whole lot of potential answers that will each require different actions to take to get you financially in the right place to address them. An advisor can answer these questions—can you? Do you want to run the risk that you will get the answers correct? In reality, "simple" never exists.

You Don't Know What You Don't Know

To further answer the "simple" question, you must ask yourself another series of questions. Almost all of us do not even know what questions to ask...we literally do not know what we are ignorant of. As a twenty-something, how many have asked themselves about their family health history as it relates to personal finance? Not many, but it's a smart question to ask, as locking in low cost disability or life insurance while young and very healthy is one of many very smart things to think about before truly significant responsibilities come to you.

For your most recent job offer, did the employer offer a matching 401(k)? If so, did you calculate the dollar value over five years of that match and compare it to another job offer to see the literal dollar value of the retirement benefit? These are things that are not intuitive to consider, and when one thinks they have a straightforward circumstance, a financial professional will bring up questions that you never would have thought of yourself.

Do You Have Dreams and Goals?

For argument's sake, let's pretend that today you are indeed very simple from a financial and wealth perspective. Do you have ambitions for the next five or ten years? Do you have visions of accomplishing something that you feel is out of touch, but would love to attempt it? Many people do, and the reality is that money and wealth impact your ability to achieve those dreams and goals.

For a personal example, in the early 1980s while in college, there was a year where I dropped down to just one class to focus on an invention I conceived. To pay for college, I did carpentry work at night and on the weekends. There was one particular task that was time consuming but needed a helper to complete. Given that I was self-employed, my preference was to not pay for a laborer to help with this task that I would be regularly doing. I invented a device to make the procedure not only easier, but a one-man job. I began researching the industry more and came to the conclusion that I could make and sell a lot of these devices to contractors and do-it-yourselfers.

My next step was to hire a patent attorney while I made the prototype. After the patent attorney concluded the search and determined I could get a utility patent, he casually said to me, "I assume you have already secured five million dollars or so to get this made in scale so the big guys don't copy and put you out of business within two years, correct?" I was very young, and clearly was not thinking ahead enough, and I said, uh, no. He suggested I save my money, not proceed with the patent and wait till I had resources. This was at a time just before patent laws got stronger and large firms could easily crush a new company by changing one tiny feature and undercutting the price by 10 percent and take the new company's share.

My dream was a solid one and had there been financial advisors that worked with younger people, or more advisors that clearly worked with entrepreneurs, I might have been able to map out a plan to raise the capital and move forward. Today, there are plenty of advisors who work with younger generations, and plenty who work with entrepreneurs. Their experience could help your dream become reality, or at minimum, connect you to likeminded people.

Your dreams and goals can be an asset, whether you are twenty-two or sixty-two. Having an objective person work with you examine how you might achieve them, despite a current lack of material assets, can be one of the best investments you ever make. Your dream might be a lifestyle, an athletic goal, a business, a public service, or political goal.

YOU CAN DO IT YOURSELF

Maybe, But...

There are self-directed investors that have done very well for themselves, and this is an undeniable fact. There is a vast amount of content available, and brokerage firms like Schwab, Fidelity, and TD Ameritrade have so much content that you can make it a full-time job to read all their information to increase your expertise.

But, there is not one professional advisor who has mastery over every wealth topic.

The most telling story that illustrates this is when Paul Sullivan of the *New York Times* wrote of his meeting as a guest at the Tiger 21 club. The club is an exclusive group whose members gather regularly to discuss all things finance and wealth. Members must have ten million dollars in investable assets and the annual dues are thirty thousand dollars. Paul wrote of his surprising experience, and in short, showed up with brokerage statements in hand expecting the group to highly criticize his investment portfolio. Instead the group of multi-millionaires pointed out he had no disability insurance, spent too much money on dog walkers and an underused vacation property, and other items that one would think are fairly pedestrian.

Paul's experience points to the notion that everyone can benefit from a coach, even if you are capable at a task. Just because you can do something capably doesn't mean that you won't benefit from coaching. Name a professional and there is a coach behind that person making him or her better.

Finally, why take the risk that there is some very beneficial aspect of wealth that you either are not aware of or miss? I'll give you another concrete example. I know of a retired, reserve military officer—a very accomplished professional in his area of expertise. He had worked in mostly large companies his entire life, but also a few small ones. Later in his life, he hired a financial advisor to do a comprehensive financial plan. He learned he could have been getting free health care from the military insurance provider, Tri-Care. He thought that as a reservist, he was not eligible, but he was. I don't know how much money he and his wife could have saved themselves and his employers over the years, but the savings might have been as much as twelve thousand dollars per year for him and his family.

We can all do things ourselves theoretically, but is it indeed being penny-wise and pound foolish? I have another personal experience that illustrates this in another way. When I bought my first home, a small ranch house, I decided to have a second story added on and to convert it to a center-hall colonial. I wanted to save as much money as I could, so I designed the addition myself. My contractor, who had re-done my kitchen before, was going to do this major addition—but asked me to hire an architect.

I resisted hiring an architect for many weeks, but the contractor kept imploring me to do so. Finally, I relented and hired an architect. My contractor was very relieved. I think the architect charged me about two thousand dollars. I do recall it not being much relative to the cost of the addition, which was six figures. What she did was added a front porch, changed the direction of the new staircase, and designed a large bay window on the back of the house. The design was simple but looked amazing. And when I compared it to what I drew up for my contractor, I felt like an idiot.

Had I not finally listened to my contractor and hired an architect, I would have been living in two ranch homes stacked on top of each other. Simply hideous. And years later when I sold the house, I made a significant profit, which I can confidently say was because of my architect's design. The house would have been livable, yes—and ugly. Hiring a professional is usually worth the expense in ways that may pleasantly surprise you.

CHAPTER 5

PROOF THAT FINANCIAL ADVISORS BENEFIT INVESTORS AND CONSUMERS

I debated adding this chapter because after all, if you have this book you already at some level believe in getting a financial advisor. However, as I was writing and talking with both advisors and consumers, both groups thought this information was necessary.

Moreover, this chapter notes some fascinating and illuminating research that can be very helpful to an investor who currently uses an advisor or who is considering a new advisor. This research can also be useful to a more substantive dialog for an existing advisor-investor relationship.

I have broken chapter into two sections. The first discusses research that quantifies the value of a financial advisor. The firms are well known, regulated institutions. The second section contains qualitative anecdotes that illustrate the benefit of an advisor.

QUANTITATIVE RESEARCH BY RESPECTED FIRMS

The research I highlight is from very large, highly regulated, respected firms. It is important to note and disclose that each of these firms markets their products and services to both individual consumers and financial advisors. A skeptic could easily say "Of course these firms are going to say financial advisors can provide a benefit; they make money from advisors!" Such a skeptic does have a point, and without a doubt, there is a conflict of interest in each of these research reports because they do in some manner make money from advisors. However, in studying the entirety of these reports, any real or perceived conflict does not in my opinion generate a less than authentic analysis. I have been in this industry for over thirty years and based on my research, these are the first such reports ever done, as opposed to reports regularly churned out by the "industry" as you may see in other fields.

The following section was originally published in *Putting a value on your value: Quantifying Vanguard Advisor's Alpha*.

VANGUARD FUNDS "ADVISORS ALPHA"

The punchline to this industry report is that Vanguard Funds "Advisors Alpha" research shows advisors can add up to a 3% increase in portfolio returns. There are many caveats to this of course, which I get into, but this work is respectable and compelling.

In September of 2016 Vanguard Funds, one of the worlds' largest mutual fund companies famous for its low-cost index funds, produced a 28-page white paper estimating that advisors who followed certain practices can add 3% more to an investment portfolio. In 2001, they created the "Vanguard Advisors Alpha" concept that by applying certain services for an advisor and by not trying to beat the market, an advisor can add up to 3% and perhaps more, to an investor's portfolio. In 2016 using this research they quantified the work into a specific number that can be achieved compared to an advisor or investor who does not employ these practices.

Vanguard uses its own "Vanguard Advisor's Alpha Strategy" which is a listing of seven different practices an advisor can takes on behalf of an investor. These practices are similar to what financial planners or wealth managers apply in their regular course of work. Vanguard stresses a number of important points about this to keep in mind:

1. The 3% will not likely be achieved every year, year in and year out. The "Advisor Alpha" will be much lower in some years, and much higher in others. Very likely some of the greatest value is during periods of market euphoria or market duress when consumers are most likely to act irrationally due to emotions.

2. The 3% increase is available to each advisor and each investor, but not every advisor will actually follow these practices, and not every consumer/investor will act on the practices the advisor recommends for them.

3. There are many other practices that advisors can perform for investors, but the seven they highlight apply to most investors.

Here are the seven practices and the performance improvement attributed to each:

Vanguard Advisor's Alpha strategy Module	Typical value added for client (basis points, 100 bps=1%)
Suitable asset allocation using broadly diversified funds/ETFs	> 0 bps*
Cost-effective implementation (expense ratios)	40 bps
Rebalancing	35 bps
Behavioral coaching	150 bps
Asset location	0 to 75 bps
Spending strategy (withdrawal order)	0 to 110 bps
Total-return versus income investing	> 0 bps*

Total potential value added About 3% in net returns

* Value is deemed significant but too unique to each investor to quantify.
Source: Vanguard.

MORNINGSTAR'S ALPHA, BETA, AND NOW... GAMMA

Morningstar is a publicly held research firm that is widely respected and used by investors, financial advisors, and institutions. In 2017 it published a research paper titled "The Value of a Gamma-Efficient Portfolio" and summarized that an average investor can increase their annual returns by 2 percent per year by using a financial advisor. It of course heavily noted in its 45-page paper that not every advisor and investor would achieve this, but this number was obtainable by adopting practices put forth in the research.

"Gamma" is the name Morningstar used for a measure to quantify the benefits of working with a financial advisor. This research focused on investing decisions alone, but did not weigh the impact of the other disciplines of financial advice, such as more prudent saving tactics, tax minimization strategies, and so forth. Morningstar pointed out that the improvement to a person's portfolio could be much higher than 2 percent when these other actions are taken into account, but in this paper focused only on the investing aspect.

At the heart of this research are seven questions the investor should ask themselves, and as you can see, there are much more complicated than simply picking the best investments for the portfolio:

1. Why invest at all?

2. Which type of account may be best?

3. What is an appropriate risk level?

4. Which asset classes should be considered?

5. How does the risk of the goal affect how I invest?

6. What investments to implement with?

7. When should the portfolio be revisited?

Each of these questions is quite complex, and when a financial advisor is asking these questions of the investor, significant thought and consideration goes into each successful reply. I found the first question quite interesting, as the research pointed out consumer scenarios where investing is not mathematically the best option. Specifically, when a consumer has high levels of high-interest debt, paying off that debt could provide better returns than investing the same money in a portfolio. In this case, a financial plan with no investment management services would benefit the consumer.

The following chart shows the percentage increase of a portfolio for each of the categories of questions asked and corresponding action taken. The chart shows three categories of investors by their relative benefit received. A low benefit investor for example is someone who is given advise for a very limited purpose such as a single 401k account when the investments are relatively limited and pre-selected. Most investors would receive the average benefit as shown below.

Benefit of Financial Advice

Question	Low	Average	High
Why Invest at All?	0.05	0.30	1.00
Which Type of Account May Be Best?	0.10	0.25	0.50
What is an Appropriate Risk Level?	0.10	0.40	1.00
What Asset Classes Should be Considered?	0.00	0.20	0.60
How Does the Risk of the Goal Affect the Portfolio?	0.05	0.20	0.50
What Investments to Implement With? — — —			
Investment Cost	0.00	0.20	0.60
Investment Quality	0.00	0.10	0.30
Tax Considerations*	0.00	0.15	0.60
When Should the Portfolio be Revisited? — — —			
Rebalancing	0.00	0.05	0.10
Investing for the Long-term	0.10	0.50	1.00
Tax Loss Harvesting*	0.00	0.10	0.50
Total	~.4	~2	**Significant**

Source: Author's calculations.

* Will not be relevant for many investors and even if so, only for a portion of the investible assets.

The Morningstar report shows a unique method of evaluating the advisor benefit, but these questions at the heart of the analysis can not only be used for justifying hiring an advisor, but can be used as a tool to better engage with an advisor that an investor has a current relationship with.

AON HEWITT AND FINANCIAL ENGINES

Aon Hewitt, a very large human resources conglomerate and Financial Engines, is an investment management firm co-founded by Nobel Prize winner Bill Sharpe. They co-produced a report that showed investors gained over 3 percent per year in net investment performance when they received "Help" with their retirement plans, specifically Defined Contribution Plans.

This research looked at over 723,000 investors retirement plans across fourteen large companies between the years 2006–2012. The total amount of these assets was fifty-five billion dollars. It compared the investors who received "help" to those that did not, and those with "help" enjoyed investment performance that was 3.32 percent higher than those that did not...and these numbers are net of fees.

The report defines "help" as the investor using either target date funds, managed accounts, or online advice. The first two investments are essentially automatic investments managed based on high level needs of the investor. While not completely a perfect comparison to an individual financial advisor, this definition is an appropriate proxy; when someone is not using one of the three above specified solutions, they are making the investment decisions themselves and are unadvised.

The data for this report comes from firms who provided retirement solutions to its employees, and in most cases, the target date funds were the default option in the plan set up, so one could argue the results have an inherent bias. However, the results are clear in that those investors who made the decision to use non "help" solutions harmed themselves as measured by investment performance.

While the AON Hewitt report is fairly different than the Vanguard and Morningstar reports, it is telling how it shows roughly the same numerical benefit of advice or "help."

Russell Investments and Envestnet are very large financial services firms that each have authored similar reports; however, these reports were only for use by financial advisors. They show added investment performance due to an advisor from 2 to 4 percent.

To sum up, there is ample research that proves the financial benefit can be achieved with a financial advisor when it comes to portfolio performance.

QUALITATIVE ILLUSTRATIONS OF ADVISOR BENEFITS

Lessons Early and Later

Her father thought buying life insurance was like "betting on death" as he used to say. Sadly, he died when Joanne (not her real name) was nineteen and her mother was thirty-nine. His passing was devastating, of course, but not having life insurance on top of not filing his taxes for the prior two years added extraordinary burden to the family he left behind, which included losing their house. They did not have an advisor at the time of his passing—moreover, Joanne's mother was not involved in the family finances at all.

Joanne's mother attended a widows' support group, where she met a female financial advisor from American Express Financial Advisors, now known as Ameriprise. The advisor gave talks about women being self-sufficient and the need to be financially literate. Joanne's mother hired the advisor, and after remarrying, they were discussing her new husband's plan for retirement from the San Francisco police force coming up in two years. The advisor had bad news for the couple: he could not afford to retire in two years as planned. The issue is that he was divorced, and his ex-wife would be entitled to half of his pension. He needed to work another seven years to contribute to his retirement plans. So, he took the advisors guidance, went back to work and saved, and seven years later in 1989, he was able to retire successfully. The plan, along with investing in the right annuity contract—one whose principal was absolutely guaranteed—secured the couple's retirement. Almost thirty years later they are still comfortably retired, and still use an Ameriprise advisor.

In 2018, Joanne now had her own challenge. She and her long-term boyfriend were grappling with issues as an unmarried couple. Issues involving assets, liabilities, sudden ill health or death, which are particularly troublesome for an unmarried couple because—for the most part—one is not recognized under law as having rights if unmarried. Particularly important for Joanne's boyfriend was his work, as he is in the arts, and his body of work would not be able to be managed by Joanne should something happen to him. The solution was to get a Domestic Partnership Trust, which afforded rights to each and allowed them the flexibility to combine and access the assets as they saw fit. While a financial advisor was not involved, Joanne shared with me that for couples at certain asset levels, her attorney strongly advised that a financial advisor should be involved with the drafting attorney for the benefit of the couple.

My Own Story

My story is somewhat common, but is proof that quality advice is worth it. My father passed away at the age of forty-five in the early 1970s, leaving six dependents: my mother, four children, and my elderly maternal grandmother who lived with us. Despite my father being an executive, he and my mother lived a lower-middle income life. We never took a family vacation, had one car and two TVs, both black and white, years later upgrading to color TVs. One of my father's friends convinced he and my mother early in their marriage that spending money on life insurance policies was the prudent thing to do when one has a family. It turned out to be incredibly sound advice.

After my father died, my mother continued to raise us as a single parent. Because of the insurance policy proceeds, she was able to be a full-time parent and focus on us. We all were raised by her through our grade school and high school years, and all but one of us got into college during this time, while our mother was able to focus exclusively on parenting by staying out of the workforce. Years later, as we all look back, we each are college educated, in our fifties, with families of our own. Aside from the twists and turns we have had as individuals, we all agree things may have been very different and much worse for one of us, or perhaps several of us, had our mother been forced to work during our early years. The great advice from an insurance agent very likely changed the course of our lives. I am very thankful as well that my parents took the great advice from that insurance agent, as they could have easily used that money for more material and immediate desires.

Planning: 140,200 Dollars Saved and a New Relationship

Marguerita (Rita) Cheng has been an advisor for nineteen years and is the CEO of Blue Ocean Global Wealth and is a Certified Financial Planner (CFP). Rita is a fervent believer in the financial planning process, so much so that if a client wants her to manage an investment portfolio, she will refuse the client unless financial planning is part of the engagement. Her firm is an independent advisory firm that does not impose stringent asset minimums and has a very diverse client base. She is a big believer in being empathetic and never judging clients, but at the same time she strives to be exceptionally detail oriented, as much as the client requires or demands.

What her clients find most surprising is how deeply personal the financial planning process is. It is not simply a computer program she fills in after getting data from a client. A client's true challenge might be incredibly personal, to the point of bring tears to hers and the client's eyes. One of her clients is a couple, who needed a financial plan to manage a major life change. The wife had a government position for years and brought in the larger salary of the two, however, she decided she needed to leave and wanted a career change to go into medicine. Their financial planning process got them through the transition, she graduated, is now in her new medical career. Even better, her new employer has even forgiven a substantial portion of her medical school debt. Changing careers was key to her personal career happiness, but the financial planning process made the transition to a one income family while returning to school a reality. These clients told Rita that with a solid plan, they no longer argue about money and are much happier. They now realize that the outcome of a solid plan is not necessarily about the money, it's about their quality of life.

Another client of hers were approaching retirement (wife was fifty-three and husband sixty-seven) and had not yet discussed what they would do should one or both fall ill. They were highly skeptical about long term care insurance. Rita coached them into thinking about the actual care, and how insurance was only one of many solutions that included family, government programs, and other options. At the end of the process it was determined that for 2,600 dollars per year, they could indeed cover the costs of long term care insurance. Thirteen years later, the husband fell ill, and that policy began paying fifty-eight thousand dollars per year in benefits to pay for his care. He needed care for three years. Had Rita not overcome the couple's skepticism, the financial loss from the care expenses would have been dramatic, particularly for the widow. The net savings of 140,200 dollars was very meaningful for this widow.

Rita shared with me that there are many surprising things about the financial planning process that consumers learn. They are shocked at how emotional it can be, because when people think financial planning, they mostly think numbers, almost like having a tax return completed. However, issues of your parent's wellness and your child's educational future are very emotional topics. Rita also wanted to share that it's never too late to find the ideal advisor for you.

One particular couple came to mind for her, and that was a couple in their seventies who changed advisors. Apparently, the advisor they had for years was clearly not interested in helping the wife get prepared for being solely responsible for the investments and related issues. They switched advisors because the husband wanted to make sure that after he was gone, his wife had the right relationship with the advisor. In fact, this husband should be applauded for his proactive nature, as the cultural norm for this generation has unfortunately been not to treat a woman the same as a man. "I'm so pleased you and Rita get along so well and that you are learning so much," the husband said. She responded, "That's because Rita actually is interested in me and what I have to say and how I feel. Our old advisor never took an interest in me."

The Qualitative Becomes Quantitative

The above three true consumer stories are in the qualitative section of this chapter, but as you can easily see, the quantitative benefits of the beneficiaries of this advice are substantive. In one story, you see a six-figure savings. In another, an ensured retirement; and lastly, a parent being able to financially care for her young children at an age where not being there runs great risk of kids getting into trouble.

The Flip Side: Self-Directed Underperformance

There are a number of studies that prove out investors on their own underperform the markets. For example, Dalbar has been producing the same study annually for over twenty years. Its "Quantitative Analysis of Investor Behavior" 2017 report shows the average equity investor underperformed the S&P 500 by 2.89 percent per year over the past twenty years. Geoffrey Friessen and Travis Sapp (of the universities of Nebraska Lincoln and Iowa State respectively) show in their research that investors underperformed by 1.56 percent from 1991–2004. There are other reports from academics such as Braverman, Dichev and Yu, and Frazzini and Lamont that each have differing numbers but share the same result that investors underperform the markets.

The conclusions about why investors underperform include investors straying from their buy and hold plan, attempting to time the market to needing the cash for some life event, then coming back to the market at the improper time.

There is no doubt that having a financial advisor will benefit a consumer, and you can illustrate the benefit with lots of high math being done as in the quantitative cases, and without deep analysis in the qualitative cases.

CHAPTER 6

WELCOME TO THE FINANCIAL ADVISOR UNIVERSE

Financial advisors are changing lives by restructuring their clients' finances. They're not only performing a transformative service; they're also educating their clients and making them willing and motivated partners in an exciting process.

Do you think it is important to understand the difference between an internist and a plastic surgeon? What a silly question, of course; not only do most people clearly know the difference—they know why they should know. These two medical professionals, while both medical doctors, perform very different services and are interested and expert in two very different things. In fact, the effects would be disastrous if you were to attempt to hire one when the other was needed.

How about the difference between divorce attorneys and real estate attorneys? Again, a seemingly inane question, but I am making the point that in financial services, there is almost as much variation in what different types of financial advisors exist and the services they offer as there is variation in medicine, law, and other professions.

It is critical that a consumer have a basic understanding of the financial advisor universe because—as you reflect on your own financial goals and aspirations you want the tools to be able to find the advisor that is perfect for you at this point in your life. You may need a different advisor in the future, or multiple advisors if your situation becomes complex, but I want to give you the ability to clearly understand the landscape and difference between them so you can choose wisely.

First, the numbers. There are over 1.7 million licensed and regulated people in the United States that can offer something that could be interpreted as financial advice of some kind. I use the term "licensed person" as this is the most common descriptor that can be used without using confusing jargon. This book is focused only on advisors that are licensed by a federal, state, or self-regulatory body. There are unregistered, private, and family office advisors that are not licensed but almost always cater only to the very wealthy. For 99 percent of Americans, only licensed persons should be considered. The industry breaks down in the following types of licensed persons: as of December 2017, there are 634,708 brokers (a person) working for 3,753 broker-dealers (a company) registered by the Financial Industry Regulation Authority (FINRA), which is a self-regulatory organization that governs broker-dealers. FINRA is authorized by the Securities and Exchange Commission, a U.S. federal government agency. There are over 120,000 investment advisor representatives (a person) on behalf of over 32,000 Registered Investment Advisers (a company), and over one point two million people who are licensed to sell insurance.

If you noticed that some of the numbers are not exact, that is because some regulators are not exactly sure how many people currently give advice or sell to consumers. This is a problem which I discuss more fully in chapter 10. Also, there are licensed persons that are registered simultaneously by three regulators and can be triple counted in the above numbers.

I will go into detail about the various sub-segments and classifications of financial advisors, but please note that these differences will blur as advisors who technically belong to one classification adopt practices used by others. I've seen this trend for a number of years and expect it to continue. In some cases, this is a positive by offering more breadth of service for the consumer, but other times, the blurring and heavy use of industry jargon makes it harder for the consumer to understand the difference in advisors. In rarer cases, an unscrupulous advisor will use this confusion to their advantage at the expense of the consumer. More on this last point in chapters 13 and 14, in which I discuss how to spot a bad advisor and how to interview an advisor.

634,708 FINRA BROKERS

This is the oldest and largest group of licensed persons that give general financial advice or sell securities such as mutual funds, stocks, bonds, and the like. They work for firms called broker-dealers that are household names like Merrill Lynch, Morgan Stanley, UBS, Wells Fargo, but also work for firms that have less-recognized names such as Raymond James, Edward Jones, and Stifel. Further still there are large numbers of licensed persons who work for firms that are rarely recognized such as LPL, Securities America, and Money Concepts, and have hundreds or even over ten thousand advisors working for them in the case of LPL.

Brokers who work for broker-dealers generally operate either as a sole advisor, or in recent years, on a team of several. Broadly speaking, they offer the advice or sell securities to their clients as they see fit, but operate under the compliance guidelines of their broker-dealer firm. They are free to recommend the security or strategy they deem the best fit for their clients, as opposed to the broker-dealer mandating a particular security or strategy, although firms do having vetting processes before any security or strategy can be offered by a broker.

Brokers, as one type of licensed professional, are allowed to sell a security to an investor. This includes stocks, bonds, options, mutual funds, and almost any other type of security. They are governed by the suitability standard meaning they must sell what is a proper recommendation for the investor, however, they are not mandated to put the clients' needs ahead of their own—called the fiduciary standard that Registered Investment Advisers, another type of licensed person—are required to do. However, a very large percentage of brokers are also representatives of a Registered Investment Adviser, and that trend is fast growing. Like many aspects of selecting your perfect financial advisor, this nuance has positive aspects and negative aspects and I'll dive into this in later chapters.

There are four broad categories of Broker Dealer firms that employ these over six hundred thousand brokers:

WIREHOUSE

The term WireHouse is industry jargon for the four largest broker-dealers; by broker count, these are: Merrill Lynch, Morgan Stanley, Wells Fargo, and UBS. The term Wirehouse stems from the origins of these firms when they were able to transmit stock quotes by telegraph over wire, which was novel in the early 1900s. What makes these firms notable is their sheer size and longevity and the broad range of products and services they offer. Each of these firms has the most substantive financial resources and can nearly literally offer any financial service a consumer would want or need. This includes retail brokerage services such as stock investing, but also acting as a Registered Investment Adviser, bringing companies public and creating new types of securities and offering banking services. These four firms have combined nearly fifty thousand brokers in every state in the U.S.

REGIONAL

Regional firms are very much like a wirehouse in terms of offering a broad range of services, with the two notable difference of not having a physical presence in every state—hence the moniker regional—and generally not offering every conceivable service like the wirehouses do. However, some regional firms are as established and financially secure as their more well-known wire competitors. For example, Janney Montgomery Scott was founded in 1832, making it more than eighty years older than Merrill Lynch. There are dozens of regionals in the United States, such as Stifel, Janney, Raymond James, and Edward Jones. There are roughly thirty thousand brokers working for regional firms.

INDEPENDENT BROKER DEALER

Independent broker dealers (IBDs) are the most different of the four types of broker dealers, but employ the largest number of brokers, at an estimated two hundred thousand-plus licensed persons. IBDs do not technically employ their brokers; rather, the brokers are contractors or franchisees, if you will. They do not get a W-2 at the end of the year, but a 1099. IBDs—unlike their wire and regional competitors—do not offer nearly every service under the sun, take companies public, have a bank or create proprietary products, or have seats on the floor of stock exchanges. IBDs offer their brokers the basic needs to the brokers, and all of the competitive access to mutual funds, stocks, bonds and strategies, but do not have corporate owned offices, ad budgets, or other overhead that the wires and regionals do. Because of this, brokers at IBDs get a much higher percentage of the revenue they generate versus their wire and regional competitors do. At most wires and regionals, the broker gets between 35–50 percent of the revenue they generate. At most IBDs, the brokers get at least 80 percent, and in some cases, more than 90 percent of the revenue. However, they pay every single cost, from rent to office supplies to computers. They are self-employed from an Internal Revenue Service perspective, and in almost every sense self-employed from a practical sense. This said, however, the broker at an IBD has far greater business freedom as the relationship between the broker-dealer and the broker is considered a vendor, rather than an employee relationship. The broker-dealer competes for brokers to come to their companies and treats them as the client.

It is very important to note that the IBD broker and broker-dealer are regulated in the same way as the wirehouse and regional firm. From FINRA's perspective there is no difference, and the IBD has the same amount of liability as the wirehouse does if one of their brokers runs afoul of regulations or harms a client.

IBDs started roughly in the 1960s, born out of the desire by established brokers to operate more independently and capture more of their revenue. These brokers felt they did not need the support from a large firm and could support their client base without office space or proprietary products and services.

LOCAL BROKER DEALER

Local broker dealers, also jargon, can have brokers that are either employees or contractors like an IBD, but are generally very small and operate in a very limited geography—usually one state. They can offer the full range of services that most other broker-dealers offer, but usually have a very niche clientele they serve, and therefore, remain small in number of brokers on staff.

Other Types of Broker-Dealer Representatives

Broker-dealers like Schwab, Fidelity, TD Ameritrade, and other firms that used to call themselves discounter firms because their commission rates were much lower than others, collectively employing tens of thousands of representatives. The licensed persons generally do not make outgoing sales calls or have clients like all other representatives do. However, in another case of the blurring of traditional roles, they employ advisors who will give an investor personal guidance and advice if and when asked.

There are other representatives that are very niche, such as institutional-only advisors, or others that do not deal directly with investors but are licensed due to technical requirements.

OVER ONE HUNDRED TWENTY THOUSAND INVESTMENT ADVISER REPRESENTATIVES

Over 120,000 licensed persons work for over thirty thousand Registered Investment Adviser (RIA) firms. These persons are called investment advisor representatives (IARs). RIAs were officially created with the Investment Advisers Act of 1940, and what primarily differentiates them from other types of licensed persons is that they are held to the fiduciary standard, meaning that they must put the needs of the clients ahead of their own. In practice, one example is that if there are two investment products that are suitable for an investor, but one that costs less to the consumer and compensates the RIA less, then the RIA must pick the one that pays the RIA less. This is just one simple example, and there are dozens more examples of the fiduciary duty in action but it makes the point. RIAs are either regulated by the Securities and Exchange Commission or their state securities regulator.

There are more than 250,000 IARS; however, many also work for FINRA broker-dealers, so for clarity sake I am only describing IARs that only work for RIAs, as opposed to IARs that also may work for a broker-dealer like Merrill or UBS for sake of categorization. In the Wall Street jargon, these are often referred to as fee-only, and because they are not also employed by a broker-dealer, cannot take a commission but do charge some type of fee based on hourly charges, fees based on assets under management, or retainer fees.

RIAs also differ from others in that each licensed person at an RIA (that is, each IAR…yes, the jargon is a killer!) almost never manages her own list of clients in a unilateral way, rather the RIA firm has an investment committee—for those RIAs that offer investment management, not all do—and only recommends what the investment committee agrees on. The IAR manages the relationship and utilizes the investment or strategies that the investment committee has approved. As an example, an IAR would never use a covered-call strategy for some of his/her clients unless the investment committee agreed that the RIA firm approved covered-call strategies.

RIAs are in all fifty states, in every major city and nearly every other city and town nationwide. They typically are small with fewer than ten employees. However, over the past ten years, many very large RIAs have emerged with hundreds of employees. Very few have a national name, but a couple that you may recognize are Fisher Investments and Edelman Financial. Their direct mail advertising, cable TV ads, and radio programs have given them some national recognition. The vast majority of RIAs however are not well known, and that can often be true in their own hometown. More on why this is important in a later chapter.

OVER ONE MILLION INSURANCE AGENTS

According to the National Association of Insurance Commissioners (NAIC), there are approximately 1.2 million active insurance agents in the United States. Each insurance agent can have different licenses authorizing them to sell various types of insurance, from fixed life insurance to car insurance to health insurance to even funeral insurance. Insurance agents are included in this book as they can offer a form of advice that is quite important to the overall financial well-being of a consumer. Increasingly, some forms of insurance are part of what is called a financial plan, and must be factored in if you hold and adhere to one of the financial planning designations.

Unlike broker-dealers and registered investment advisers, there is no national regulator of insurance agents, so exact numbers of insurance agents are not reliably found. Each state regulates their own insurance agents, but the NAIC, which is essentially a trade association of the state regulators, offers helpful data.

BROAD CATEGORIES OF WHAT ADVISORS DO

There are broad categories of what service a financial advisor performs, and it is imperative to have a basic understanding of each broad service as a starting point. Some of these terms are industry jargon and advisors never use that moniker to describe themselves. Some terms are used readily in advisor marketing. I will define each broad term and share which term is jargon, and which is widely accepted by most advisors. I will also share why knowing these terms are important when selecting an advisor for you.

ASSET MANAGER

A financial advisor who is an asset manager is focused solely on investing in securities such as stocks, bonds, mutual funds, and alternative assets and similar investments. They do not offer services like financial planning, life insurance, taxes, or what is currently called wealth management. These advisors are singularly focused on investing your money and achieving a rate of return, based on your specific needs of acceptable investment risk and timeline. They make decisions to invest in a specific stock or bond. For example, an asset manager may strongly prefer to invest in Exxon stock for your portfolio over Mobil for various reasons.

There are asset managers who specialize in one type of securities, such as stocks or bonds. They spend their entire careers following the particular market they are interested in and accrue a portfolio of securities that they believe are best for clients. Asset managers sometimes use this term, sometimes just use the term financial advisor, or investment advisor. The term asset manager is not a regulated term and therefore is jargon.

EXAMPLE: A FOCUS ON ANALYSIS

Jim Thibault has always had a love of finance, so much so that while he was studying for his MBA, at the suggestion of his professor, he decided to leave a twenty-year engineering career for financial services. After a two-year stint at Smith Barney, he co-founded wealth management firm Barron Financial with CPA Tom Barron. Twelve years later, Jim is running the firm with a mission to provide a level of asset management service that is typically not available to those with portfolios between 250,000 to one million dollars.

Jim's engineering background and analytical skills have served him and the firm well. With eighty-five clients and very low client turnover, Jim is focused on giving an exceptional level of attention to his clients' portfolios. He invests client funds mostly in mutual funds, and sometimes exchange traded funds (ETFs). In some asset classes, he uses active mutual funds, in others, he applies passive funds. Based on the global economy, he will make strategic or tactical investment decisions. Jim utilizes significant mathematical models as part of his investment process and will spend considerable time with his clients explaining his method to ensure that they understand his reasoning for making investment decisions.

As an analytical person, Jim spends as much as four hours per day researching and evaluating trends to better understand how to improve portfolio performance for his clients. Jim said that one of the more surprising things his clients learned about engaging Barron Financial is how much time Jim spends with the client explaining their investments. But not only the proposed portfolio changes—Jim takes a great deal of time to help the client understand what investments they currently had from a prior advisor, as many investors are not fully aware of their own portfolios.

Most of Barron Financial's clients have come from referrals and interestingly, the firm has a large representation of women who are either divorcees or widows versus other demographic groups. In our meeting, Jim attributed this to his perspective that he truly wants his clients to understand the investment process and goes about the education process in a non-patronizing manner. Survey after survey has shown that firms that adopt these professional standards will continue to appeal to investors of all backgrounds.

ASSET GATHERER

An asset gatherer, which is jargon, is very similar to an asset manager. However, the big difference is that instead of selecting individual stocks, bonds, or mutual funds, the advisor picks other financial advisors who are asset managers. The reason why some are asset gatherers is the belief that a financial advisor should pick the very best asset manager, as there are so many of them to choose from. Asset gatherers never refer to themselves as such, but it is critical to recognize when an advisor outsources asset management to another. In addition, the model of using other asset managers is one born from the "management consulting" concept, where large pension funds would divide up their money amongst a number of asset managers to reduce risk. They needed an advisor to help them select and monitor the underlying manager.

FINANCIAL PLANNER

A financial planner is someone who creates a written plan covering dozens of financial topics including taxes, insurance, investments, retirement, cash flow, savings, and so forth. A financial plan is a complex and lengthy document that is essentially a blueprint for a consumer's total financial picture. The term financial planner is not regulated, but rather, some states will regulate someone who offers financial planning services. A financial planner can write the plan and either implement or not implement the plan, making the investments and buying the insurance suggested in the plan.

EXAMPLE: ADVICE, NOTHING BUT ADVICE

Jim Ludwick is a financial planner who either charges by the hour or by the specific project. He does not charge asset management fees to run a portfolio nor does he sell securities for a commission. For an hourly rate, Jim and his firm, MainStreet Financial Planning, create an incredibly detailed financial plan for you. They do the dirty work, such as actually reading your insurance policies—to determine how your financial future would be impacted should a disaster strike—as just one example.

Jim has been providing only advice by the hour for sixteen years, and when he started, charged just 150 dollars per hour. When I interviewed Jim, he shared that after other careers, including asset management and commercial real estate, he found Sheryl Garrett's firm—Garrett Planning Network—which trains advisors to be hourly advice-givers catering to middle America. Jim went through the training and was advisor number 113 to take Sheryl's coursework. Jim purposefully named his company to send a message that advice was available to everyone. His firm has grown significantly, and due in large part to referrals and now has offices in California, New York, Maryland, and Washington D.C. He often works remotely and, in fact, 80 percent of his clients now meet with him via phone or webcam. He has a team that charges different project fees based on complexity of the client's needs.

The most surprising things Jim's clients have about his advice is how very specific it is for investments, insurance, and all aspects of their financial lives. For example, with one client, Jim realized the client's insurance coverage for water and sewer damage was far too low. He told the client he must increase the coverage—and of course the premium goes up—but if disaster strikes, the client is covered. Jim noted that far too many people read their insurance policy after they need to make a claim, which is too late. Any investment or financial plan requires the client be involved in some capacity, or to a high degree in the case of financial planning. Clients must sign off on agreements, such as changing brokerage agreements, IRAs, and insurance policies. When he started tracking it, Jim found that only 50 percent of his clients actually followed through on the great advice. For an advisor, that is not only a frustrating reality; it can be saddening because the client is literally harming themselves and paying for the very advice they ignore. Jim encouraged a software developer to create an email follow-up system with literal color-coded action buttons that are green, blue, and yellow, to make it easier to nudge a client into action. Now his clients have an implementation rate over 80 percent.

There are consumers who shun the concept of paying for a financial plan solely because of the outlay of money. I asked Jim what he says to these people. "It's simple. I ask them to share the biggest financial pain they have ever experienced. Then I ask them if they paid for a plan that avoided this pain, would that expense have been worth it?" Jim said. "For example, in retrospect, do you think your actions during the market correction of 2008 would have been different had you had someone like me guiding you?" Almost always, he says, they say yes.

WEALTH MANAGER

Wealth manager is industry jargon, but most in the industry agree that it is someone that does both financial planning and asset management or asset gathering. Wealth management is one of the fastest growing, services as it encompasses every aspect from the financial plan to making the investments in funds or stocks and bonds.

In the asset management function of a Wealth manager's job, this person can create a portfolio of securities that include stocks, bonds, and alternative investments. Alternative investments are generally those that are not your standard stock, bond, or mutual fund comprised of the two. They can be options, hedge funds, or real estate. The benefit is both the opportunity to have investments that don't go up and down in value in lockstep with the market, and the potential for higher rates of return.

The nuances of what an advisor can do are often lost in investors. Real estate investing is one of those things that many people do not think their advisor would opine on, however, the reality is real estate is an asset class that most advisors have in their consideration set for a client, depending upon the needs and specifics of the client.

ASSET CLASSES-ONE EXAMPLE

A.J. Chivetta is a veteran real estate expert and the CEO of Selequity, a technology platform that makes it much easier for advisors to recommend commercial real estate for their clients. A.J. explained how his platform works, and in general, how private real estate investing is accessed by advisors. In 2012, the JOBS Act was passed, which—among other things—gave both large and small investors better access to real estate investments that were, in the past, only available to high net worth investors with connections in the real estate industry. Selequity enables financial advisors to select pre-vetted, non-publicly traded commercial real investments managed by some of the best property operators in the country.

Non-publicly traded commercial real estate as an investment has not only outperformed some other asset classes, it generally is uncorrelated to the stock markets making it an appealing asset in a client's portfolio. The investor is buying a percentage of the legal entity that owns the property, also known as a private placement. Of course, commercial real estate can be invested in via a mutual fund or a trust that trades on an exchange, but those have always been available to anyone and can get whipsawed in price by the market fluctuations. They also don't have other advantages, such as making a specific investment in one property or investing in a specific area of the country.

A financial advisor guides an investor through the three basic questions when evaluating the investment. First, what is the type of property? Options include multi-tenant residential properties, to retail buildings renting to a Walgreens for example, to new development projects like a new condo community. Second, what is the property manager's strategy? Is it to add value to an existing property or is it a long-term development plan? Third, what is the property manager's expertise, history and pedigree? Thanks to the convergence of both the 2012 JOBS

Act and advanced technology, financial advisors today can bring investing in private real estate to investors that in the past was nearly impossible. Previously, you either had to be a high net worth investor or you had to have local contacts to be aware of projects that were raising capital.

RETIREMENT AND BENEFIT PLAN ADVISOR

There are advisors that focus on retirement plans such as 401(k)s offering their services to the employer to select the plan legal documents, the investments, and the ongoing monitoring. While most advisors may have one or two retirement plans, it is a specialty, and by some estimates there are only a few thousand advisors whose clients are primarily retirement plans. This term also is jargon, but most advisors will identify themselves as such.

SECURITIES SALES PERSON

This is a licensed person who primarily sells a security to an investor. The regulatory term is registered representative. The industry was almost exclusively securities sales persons, also referred to as brokers, but in the last thirty years, a large percentage of licensed persons migrated to planning, asset gathering, or asset management. The term securities sales person is never used by a licensed person, as it is jargon. There is nothing wrong with a person selling securities as their chosen career if that is clear to the consumer.

Most people would agree that in retrospect, if someone sold them Apple stock, Microsoft stock, or Facebook stock in the first couple of years of those companies' history, they would be quite pleased with the results. This said, history shows it is incredibly difficult to pick these at the right time. Nonetheless, these companies and others depended on early investors to make them what they are today. Imagine if no one was brave enough to sell these stocks in those early days and no one was brave enough to buy them?

MULTIPLE ROLES AND MULTIPLE FIRM TYPES

A licensed person can perform one or several of the above functions, and often do. For example, any licensed person for a broker-dealer is, by definition, authorized to be a securities salesperson. However, in practice, they may have only acted as an asset gatherer for their entire career, selecting the optimal asset managers for a client.

A financial planner can work for an RIA or can work for a wirehouse. Virtually any service can be performed at any type of firm with some exceptions. I'll go into this complexity in later chapters and how it's relevant to advisor selection.

NICHE CATEGORIES OF ADVISORS

Once you become aware of the broad categories, it can be profoundly valuable to you as a consumer to know there are narrow and niche categories of what advisors do and for whom. While most advisors are generalists, there are many thousands of advisors that cater to a niche. If you are a member of that niche, you will experience a level of service and satisfaction that generally is greatly superior to a generalist. For example, there are wealth managers who exclusively cater to medical doctors, as medical doctors have issues that only pertain to them—such as insurance, retirement, and partner issues. If you are doctor, an advisor who fully understands your business can provide value far and above a generalist wealth manager. In another example, there are advisors that are expert in a kind of employee benefit plan called an Employee Stock Ownership Plan (ESOP). If you are either an employee or the owner of a company that qualifies for an ESOP, an advisor who is expert in ESOPs can build wealth for you that otherwise would not be likely.

CLIENT NICHE

Occupational Niche

There are niche advisors for almost every imaginable occupation. For example, in 1996 I had an advisor client at Waterhouse Securities, the predecessor to TD Ameritrade. This advisor specialized in serving lobster fisherman, and the firm owner would literally walk down to the docks to meet the boats where his clients came in from a long period of time at sea. After selling their catches, he would assist them in completing forms to invest in the mutual funds and open accounts and related tasks to ensure the fisherman were investing appropriately.

CRNA Financial Planning is a firm that caters to certified registered nurse anesthetists, as their career particulars can involve business formation, planning, and tax issues that are unique to their profession.

Mainstay Capital Management, LLC in Michigan manages the retirement investments of thousands of auto industry workers, as it has deep knowledge of how the auto industry pension plans work.

RAA is an investment advisor in Texas that caters to airline pilots and has over three thousand pilots as clients. The employee benefits of an airline pilot are unique, as is their psyche so these combined facts create a valuable service if you are in this career.

Considering a financial advisor who caters to your chosen career or profession can yield substantial benefits. When an advisor understands your unique industry, you will spend less time educating your advisor on the nuances of your situation, and moreover, he or she will likely educate you on finer aspects of financial guidance that you may not be aware of. Lastly, your advisor will be able to share back with you best practices of how peer professionals have improved their financial lives.

Generational and Gender Niches

Much has been written about the psychology of different generations and research has shown that Boomers, Gen Y, and Millennials do have different attitudes toward risk, how they want to be served, and savings. Thankfully there are advisory firms that cater to various generations. Firms like oXYGen Financial in Georgia cater to Gen X and Gen Y; this particular firm was started in 2008 to cater to the overstressed generation that was spooked by the year's financial events. XY Planning Network is a network of hundreds of planners that don't have minimums and cater to the cost-conscious younger client that needs help getting started.

There are many firms that cater to woman investors such as Resource Consulting Group in Florida and Fish and Associates Financial Services in Tennessee. These firms focus on female clients because many women have felt left out of the financial conversation but, paradoxically, now influence the financial decisions of the household more than ever.

Affinity Niche

There are many firms that cater to those that have served in the military. For example, USAA is a very large insurance carrier and mutual fund company, but it also has licensed staff to give personal financial advice. The Burney Companies. based in Virginia. for many of its early years catered to military officers. Briaud Financial Advisors—based in College Station, Texas, where Texas A&M University is located—focused on those in academia in its earlier years and now also focuses on doctors. The LGBTQ community has unique needs ranging from marriage, to employer benefits to parental issues. There are many firms around the country that cater to this group; for example, The Millstone Evans Group of Raymond James in California has been active for several years with this niche.

Life Stage

Going through a life-changing event such as divorce, the death of a spouse, or recent retirement, wreaks havoc on a person. The financial impacts on a person are often not intuitive and at this extremely emotional time in a person's life, the financial repercussions can easily be overlooked. It is not uncommon that big mistakes are made at this point. Most advisors who cater to someone in a new life stage often counsel to do nothing at all different following such an emotional event.

There are of course specific exceptions to this, such as getting a death certificate so the life insurance payment can be made, as one very specific example. However, there are hundreds of advisors around the country that specialize in a life-stage change event. Their counsel can be invaluable as they have clients that have gone through exactly what you have just experienced, and they know what issues you will face. Of equal importance, advisors won't have the emotional stress you will have, making it easier to avoid mistakes due to emotion or ignorance. There are advisors that cater to those recently divorced, widowed, and retired. The category of advisors catering to retirees is broad as most advisors have retirees as clients, so more care is needed to home in on an advisor that has very deep experience dealing with recently retired people. That will be covered in the chapter that deals with how to find an advisor and the chapter on how to interview and question an advisor.

For example, Alexandra Armstrong is the founder of Armstrong, Fleming & Moore, Inc. and has been working with widows for quite some time. In fact, in 1993 she wrote a book about the topic with Mary Donahue titled, *On Your Own: A Widow's Passage to Emotional and Financial Well-Being*. The book is now on its fifth printing. Alexandra has been in the industry fifty years, is a highly regarded advisor, and also involved in the pro bono planning effort.

Service and Expertise Niche

There are specific advisor services or specialties that can encompass the large part—or all of—of an advisor's client base. If you are a consumer with a special situation, you will find significant value in seeking out advisors that have expertise in these areas.

Employee Stock Ownership Plans (ESOPS)

ESOPs are an amazing type of retirement plan that benefits both the employer and the employee, but they are among the most complicated type of plan that exists. Advisors that guide business owners on ESOPs are invaluable. If you know of a business owner, please read on and share with your friend, as you may be doing them a big favor. According to the United States census bureau, there are about 5.4 million private businesses. The National Association of Employee Ownership states there are only 9,615 ESOPs, so even if a modest percentage of them qualify for an ESOP, there are still many thousands of businesses that could be enjoying these unique benefits.

ESOPs Plans were authorized by the Department of Labor in the 1970s to encourage more employee ownership of smaller private companies by giving major tax breaks to the owners of the companies who set up the plans. I interview an ESOP expert in the next chapter, but it's such a beneficial tool its worth mentioning twice in this book.

I have benefited from ESOPs twice in my life. First as an employee; second, later in life as a CEO setting one up for my employees. I was very fortunate as in the former case I was able to purchase my first home with my ESOP money, and in the latter, I took great pride knowing employees financially benefitted from owning stock in the company.

Concentrated Stock Positions

If you work for a company and have received significant stock as part of your compensation, most of your wealth may be concentrated in that one company. It is never a good to have all your eggs in one basket goes the saying. There are advisors that are expert in methods to reduce your wealth risk.

Lump Sum/Suddenly Wealthy

Most people fantasize about winning the lottery, inheriting money from that rich uncle, or cashing out from their next dot com app and living happily ever after. The reality is that a disturbing percentage of people who receive lump sums do not handle the money well. The *New York Times* published an article years ago about ten lotto winners, eight of them declaring bankruptcy just several years later. A significant percentage of retired NFL players also face bankruptcy within five years. While NFL players are not receiving one lump sum, many retire while relatively young and never expected to have that kind of money growing up. Managing a lump sum comes with many unique issues, such as tax, saving, interest rate, and other considerations. Frivolous spending is what sinks most in this situation.

Special Needs Children

For parents of children with special needs, the financial impact can be devastating, and as such, working with a financial advisor who is experienced in these areas can be vital. A special needs child who was born with a condition can have different financial implications than that of a child who has developed a condition due either to a medical condition or accident.

Intergenerational Wealth Transfer/Family Businesses

For those families that are fortunate enough to have inherited wealth, there are issues that can be very stressful and financially challenging. Mismanagement of these issues can have a variety of ills ranging from massive tax bills for heirs, to unknown risks, to family disputes that can destroy relationships for years. The expertise needed to shepherd a family includes both the technical and the emotional. For example, someone I met was part of a family that inherited property that was once a farm, but now is a weekend retreat for an extended family of siblings, aunts, uncles, and cousins.

PROFESSIONAL AND INDUSTRY DESIGNATIONS

Many financial advisors hold designations that show they have taken additional study to be more knowledgeable in a particular area. There are actually close to 200 designations that exist, with more being created every year. Designations are granted by private organizations, not government bodies that are most often non-profits. These bodies were formed by industry professionals to further the industry by creating coursework and requirements to show competency in a particular field.

In the following section, I have interviews with some of the senior executives of organizations that grant designations. I selectively conducted these interviews not to single out any one group, but rather because their history is informative as to the depth of education that some advisors undertake, which I think most investors do not fully appreciate. Following these interviews are links to FINRA, which provide details to all the designations and directions and how to understand them.

INVESTOR ADVOCACY

Paul Smith is the President and CEO of the CFA Institute, the oldest and largest professional membership body for the investment management industry. It grants the Chartered Financial Analyst (CFA) designation, which Paul received in 2001. Paul was born and raised in London, has been in the investment management industry for most of his thirty-seven-year professional career including positions in Hong Kong, Paris, and now Charlottesville, Virginia, where the CFA Institute is based.

The CFA Institute has over 150,000 members in 160 countries, of which over 69,000 are in the U.S. It is best known for its CFA designation, which is considered to be the most arduous and most valued credential in the industry. Four years of relevant experience is a prerequisite, and the exam is administered in three sections over the course of three years. Paul explained that while the institute is well known for the CFA designation, most of its actual work is spent on thought leadership, advocacy, and policy making—all to make the industry better. Paul stressed that the institute is not a lobby group, rather an association of individuals that endeavors to put the client back in focus as the reason to exist. The organization has roots going back to 1929 when the first security analyst society was founded, and serving the client was the guiding star. This was also the beginning of the age of famed value investor Benjamin Graham, whose most well-known student at Columbia Business School was Warren Buffett.

The Institute's advocacy is to try and help high net worth investors understand who to trust. Over the last thirty years or so, the industry has lost credibility and needs to regain its sense of purpose to serve the client. Paul explained that this drift away from client focus began years ago when investment firms that were partnerships became very large corporations, many publicly held, and the pull of corporate profitability distracted the industry from serving the client above all else.

When an advisor has a CFA designation, the investor knows several things. First, it shows the advisor has a high level of technical competence in investment management, whether the investments are fixed income, equities, domestic, or international. Second, each CFA Charterholder must sign an annual declaration to uphold the CFAI professional conduct code, which is based on business ethics. Finally, the Institute has staff to investigate any investor complaints of improper conduct and will expel anyone found to violate the conduct requirements. In Paul's opinion, the average high net worth investor needs both an investment management professional (a CFA), a financial planning professional (a CFP), and likely a CPA and attorney to cover all the aspects of wealth management.

PROFESSIONAL DESIGNATIONS MATTER

According to FINRA, there are 183 financial services professional designations, but only eight of them are accredited by the two independent certifying bodies. In my discussion with Sean Walters, the CEO of the Investments and Wealth Institute, formerly IMCA (Investment Management Consultants Association) he said that multiple studies illustrated the confusion investors have about designations, and that in particular, high net worth investors are very interested in understanding how any specific designation applies to their needs.

The Institute is a thirty-three-year-old professional education and standards association and is one of only a few organizations to have an accredited designation, its CIMA designation. The institute's founding was around the concept of portfolio construction and advancing higher standards of learning and conduct around that expertise. The CIMA was originally designed for institutional clients. For example, an institution like a large university endowment or a municipality wants to ensure that the investments not only achieve certain investment return benchmarks, but that the risks to the investments are minimized. In the process of selecting the correct asset managers to whom to allocate money, the CIMA designation shows the institution a high level of competence in this endeavor. In later years, high net worth and ultra-high net worth individuals and families sought out this level of professionalism as well. This led to the creation of the Certified Private Wealth Advisor certification, which is an advanced competency for financial planners and private wealth advisors who work with high-net-worth clients.

There are over twelve thousand CIMA holders, about a third of them from the "Wirehouse" firms of Merrill Lynch, Morgan Stanley, Wells Fargo, and UBS. Another third are RIA and independent firms, and the final third comes from regional firms, banks, and institutional managers themselves. Sean believes an advisor that illustrates the desire for higher education and life-long learning ,and holds himself or herself to stringent independent standards—such as a CIMA holder—provides a significant value to investors.

In addition to competence, the ability to be a steward of the investor's financial future is vital. "Investors need to distance themselves from their own fear and biases," stated Sean, and moreover, they sometimes need to "turn the keys over to their designated financial driver, as they are often aware their own inability to deal with risk can hurt them."

NINETY-ONE YEARS OF ACADEMIA

Michael Finke, Ph.D., CFP® is the Dean and Chief Academic Officer at The American College of Financial Services. He received a doctorate in consumer economics from Ohio State University in 1998 and in finance from the University of Missouri in 2011. In our conversation about The American College, he shared a very interesting perspective on The College, and in fact, on the very history of educating financial advisors.

The College was founded in 1927 by Solomon S. Huebner, intending to professionalize the sales of life insurance. It is the oldest institution that trains financial advisors in the United States. Prior to the existence of The College, life insurance sales were made in a variety of inconsistent manners. The Wild West could be an accurate descriptor of the time. However, by the 1950s the professionalism in the insurance sales industry grew to the point where cash value life insurance was the predominant product for the middle class. In fact, in the 1950s, most middle-income families could not affordably invest in stock and bonds. This vehicle offered unique benefits, including both the attributes of an investment and the risk mitigation feature of a lump sum payout in the case of an untimely death. By the late 1970s and 1980s, the availability of mutual funds and defined contribution retirement plans like 401ks allowed middle income families to more easily get access to stock and bond investments. Cash value life became used more often by the wealthy as a specialized planning tool.

Michael made this observation: the barriers to entry in the financial services industry can be low, with some licensed persons being required to only take a fairly simple exam to work with the public. When an advisor has a professional designation from The College, be it a CLU or ChFC or other College designation, it tells the investor that this advisor has taken advanced course work the equivalent of eight college level classes. It demonstrates deep knowledge and specialization in financial planning. For example, the ChFC is a very similar designation to the CFP, but with additional applied practical teachings in areas such as divorce planning, as one example. The American College has the largest faculty of educators of any organization, providing dedicated training of financial services education. An advisor that has a designation from the College demonstrates an interest and dedication to higher education that an uncredentialed advisor will have difficulty illustrating.

A UNIQUE PERSPECTIVE

Robert (Bob) Johnson, PhD, CFA®, CAIA®, CLF®, was the President and CEO of The American College of Financial Services. If the American College name does not ring a bell, designations offered by the institution such as Chartered Life Underwriter (CLU®), Chartered Financial Consultant (ChFC®) and Retirement Income Certified Professional (RICP®) may be familiar. These are three popular designations that this non-profit educational institution offers, and many tens of thousands of advisors hold College credentials.

In my discussion with Bob, he explained that the CLU was the only designation The College offered in its first fifty-four years, but as the industry started to move towards financial planning, The College added additional designations. The school now offers eight professional designations and has over one hundred thousand advisors who have completed at least one of these programs.

Bob has a fascinating background and perspective. He has been a life-long learner and has dedicated his career to practical financial education. He earned his PhD in investments from the University of Nebraska, taught for many years at Creighton University, and spent sixteen years at the CFA Institute where he led all aspects of the CFA Program. His tenure at the American College has afforded him the opportunity to expand on what he calls "Pracademia"—the intersection of practical, applied knowledge and academic rigor.

In our discussion, Bob told me that one of his high school classmates was Peter Buffett, son of famed investor Warren Buffett. The elder Buffett is "my true north" Bob explained, thanks to Buffett's long term, pragmatic approach to investing. When it comes to investing and planning, Bob is passionate, believing that consumers going into it completely alone is as dangerous as people self-administering medical procedures.

"It may seem counterintuitive, but institutional money management is actually much easier than managing the financial affairs of a typical individual investor. Retail investors can interject in the process, dictate direction that is not founded in research, and become emotional to the point of needing to be talked off the ledge," Bob told me. "In fact, I believe that the most important function of financial advisors is to educate clients and hold their hands during tumultuous market periods."

According to Bob, increasing longevity might be one of the most important, and frankly daunting, issues facing investors today and in the coming years. For example, the College created the RICP designation to help train advisors on the decumulation phase of retirement. Over 5,400 practicing advisors have earned this credential in its first five years of existence. Social Security claiming strategies are very complicated, drawing down say 4 percent of your assets each year is no longer a number we can bank on, considering any one of us could live ten or more years longer than the actuarial tables predict. All of these factors, and many more, make the decumulation stage even more complicated than the accumulation stage. The number one fear of retirees is outliving their money, a fate no one wants to face.

"This profession, and my past position at the American College, allowed me to play a role in helping improve peoples' financial security and, thus their lives," Bob said. "Most advisors have precisely the same mindset."

FINRA WEBSITE AND DESIGNATION SEARCH TOOL

I encourage you to put down the book, grab your phone or computer, and visit this website: http://www.finra.org/investors/professional-designations

First, this site is operated by FINRA, the broker-dealer self-regulator, and while I could have included this information with a citation, this site is totally independent and updated regularly. Moreover, it has a terrific comparison tool where you can compare up to three designations at a time. For now, go to the site, and if you recognize any designations, click on the name and review it. There is very informative data on these designations.

Some advisors do overuse a designation in their marketing, particularly when that designation is quite easy to obtain. Conversely, there are designations that are very difficult to obtain; it is meaningful to you, the investor, that your advisor show competence in a particular area of expertise. There are a few things to look for in a quality designation. First, what are the pre-requisites? Second, what are the education requirements? Third, are there continuing education requirements? Fourth, is there an investor complaint process? A small number of designations are accredited, which is a very high standard. In general, the greater the education, prerequisite, and continuing education requirements, the more stringent the designation. Of course, if an advisor can lose the designation via investor complaint process, then the designation has even more meaning.

SECURITIES INDUSTRY LICENSES

Securities industry licenses are granted by state government departments, or by Self-Regulatory Organizations (SRO's). Unlike designations, they are mandatory and a pre-requisite for being in the particular field of securities or insurance. Every person must have some sort of securities industry license, although there are some exemptions which are rare. Some exams are difficult, such as the Series 7, which covers a very broad topic range of securities and takes about six hours to complete and many months of preparation. Others are relatively easy, such as the Series 63, which focuses largely on interstate regulation and takes only thirty minutes to take with a couple hours of preparation.

Licenses are less impressive or relevant to an investor as compared to designations. Any advice giver must have the Series 65 or Series 66, and anyone selling a security must have the Series 7 or Series 6. The industry trains advisors to pass theses exams, as opposed to truly learning the information such as in a designation. To be fair, the exams do include a lot information that is not practical for everyday advice giving.

CHAPTER 7

THE PUBLIC IS LARGELY UNINFORMED ABOUT FINANCIAL ADVISORS

Consumers from all walks of life—even those at the highest income and wealth levels—are often unaware of the financial advisory community.

There have been several research studies showing that investors are uninformed and confused about financial advisors. There is so much confusion about advisors, in fact, that the confusion must be broken down by the type of confusion and the reason for that confusion.

"COMPETING" REGULATORS GENERATE CONFUSION

The well-known Rand Report commissioned in 2008 by the Securities and Exchange Commission focused on the confusion between broker-dealers representatives and Registered Investment Advisers. In short, broker-dealer representatives are held to a suitability standard, which means they must recommend an investment that is suitable...but not necessarily the best for the client. The fiduciary standard, on the other hand, must be followed by Registered Investment Advisers; this type of advisor must recommend what is best for the client, even if it means the advisor makes less money because of it. It's a higher standard. Certain regulators, industry groups, and advisors themselves, have been debating for years that these two standards apply to two groups competing with each other. Yet they offer the same service, which is terribly confusing to the investor. Most investors are not aware of the difference, and that was shown clearly by the Rand Report of 2008.

To make matter worse, more and more often, firms can be both a Registered Investment Adviser (RIA) and a broker-dealer representative, which can make it more confusing to the consumer. On top of this, the Department of Labor recently created rules governing retirement accounts mandating that any licensed person advising a retirement account must apply the Fiduciary Standard, regardless if they are a broker-dealer or RIA. Not all the rules have been implemented yet, and as of this date, the current administration has delayed implementation. This too has yielded greater confusion and ignorance.

A 2017 Scottrade retirement study yet again reveals investor confusion. Forty-three percent of the respondents who use an advisor say they don't always know why they have the retirement investments they have. Multiple other responses in this survey show dissatisfaction or confusion about conflicts with the advisor and their recommendations.

FAMOUS, WEALTHY PEOPLE CAN BE IGNORANT TOO

The ignorance of financial advisors is not limited to laymen. Sometimes very well-known people with significant followers are uninformed. Take for example this tweet by famous author Robert T. Kiyosaki, of *Rich Dad Poor Dad: What The Rich Teach Their Kids About Money—That The Poor and Middle Class Do Not!* fame:

"Financial planners are henchmen for banks and mutual funds. They sell you their products, take your money, charge you fees, and use your money to get richer. #financialeducation" (Source: @theRealKiyosaki, January 24, 2018.)

There are many things that are patently wrong about his statement. First, very few financial planners work for a bank or mutual fund. Some do, but the vast majority work either for a Registered Investment Adviser that is fee-only, meaning they literally and operationally cannot sell a fund or they work for a broker-dealer that has the ability to offer or sell virtually every type of investment possible, mutual funds just being one of many options. Using the term "henchman" evokes the image of a hulking brute in a black coat, baseball bat in hand, employed by the bank or mutual fund brutalizing investors. This is simply not the case, and in fact, is *never* the case.

Secondly, Kiyosaki is ignorant of the fact that there are thousands of financial planners that neither sell anything or even recommend a specific investment. What they do is create a financial plan for a flat fee or monthly fee, notably not for selling or recommending a product in any way shape or form. These plans can range from five hundred dollars to two thousand dollars or more, depending on the person or family complexity. Financial plans encompass cash flow, insurance, retirement, taxes, and many other financially related topics. There are over seventy-five thousand Certified Financial Planners (CFP) in the U.S. who take stringent exams, must take annual continuing education courses, and face expulsion if they break the rules governing CFP conduct. They are covered in greater detail later.

The part of the tweet that states financial planners "use your money to get richer" is frankly, wildly ignorant. I have personally met thousands of financial planners at trade shows, events, and in person, during my thirty-year career. The vast majority of financial planners are themselves either middle income or upper middle income. While some have become rich by building very large planning practices, most are not. If you apply common sense, it's very hard to get rich by offering five hundred- to two-thousand-dollar plans, especially when it takes many hours of labor to produce a plan.

Having a financial plan completed for you by a competent, third-party expert is one of the best investments one can make. It is next to impossible for most people to garner such expertise to create a plan on their own, and of course Kiyosaki's tweet does not speak to the benefit of a financial plan, or even to the existence of a thing called a financial plan.

Finally, it is damaging that he uses the "#financialeducation" hashtag in his tweet. As of the date of this writing, on his Twitter public description of himself, he states "Financial Education Advocate." His tweet misinforms the reader, and I sincerely hope that not too many of his then 1.4 million followers read this tweet or took it to heart. I reached out to Kiyosaki twice that day and requested he delete or modify the post, but never received a reply.

This misinformation by such a well-known public person is another objective proof point that many are uninformed about financial advisors. You, the reader, are certainly not alone.

2011 STUDY BY THE SECURITIES AND EXCHANGE COMMISSION

This 208-page study required by the Dodd-Frank Act pointed to many areas of confusion by the investing public. It outlines that investors are confused by designations that are used by advisors, by the difference that RIAs and BD reps are regulated differently. It pointed out that investors believe that all advisors put their clients' interests first, although the varying rules do not require all advisors to do so, only RIAs, and not BD reps.

The report quoted a prior report paid for by the SEC in 2006 to the Rand Corporation to determine a number of things about the industry, one being the level of general understanding by the investing public. Investors mostly do not understand advisors, and interestingly found that the advisory firms felt that their clients trusted them without really understanding what they did. Two-thirds of the investors surveyed were experienced investors.

Also mentioned was a CFA Institute survey of investors that asked various questions about their understanding of broker-dealer reps and RIAs, and not surprisingly, the respondents failed to recognize the basic differences between different types of financial professionals.

SECRETS THAT SHOULD NOT BE

"The best-kept secret in the United States Tax Code that can positively impact a business owner are ESOPs..." says Don Israel, the co-founder of New York based Benefit Concepts Systems, Inc. He and partner Dave Weinstock started the firm in 1984, and although Don is a CPA and teaches continuing education for CPAs, his focus is on full service ESOP consulting. For full disclosure, I hired Don and his firm in years past to set up an ESOP, but I am not a current client.

ESOPs are an amazing way for a small business owner to cash out part or all of his or her business, and financial advisors play an important role in the process. They are very complicated, however, which is one of many reasons why even so-phisticated business people are not aware of them. First, let's discuss the benefits of an ESOP. This unique retirement plan allows a privately held business owner to sell their company, or a part of it—as little as 30 percent of it—and never pay capital gains taxes on the sale.

The owner is essentially selling the company to its employees. The employees do not write a check for the shares—rather, a trust is set up and money is borrowed based on the company's profitability. The employees get the stock for free in a special, additional retirement account. For the business owner, it can be a huge relief that they have a friendly buyer and don't have to pay an investment banker, and as long as the firm is sold for its fair value, as determined by an independent valuation firm. Also, the seller can maintain management control of the company, which can be a terrific boon for companies that have multiple generations working there. According to industry statistics, ESOP companies grow between 8 and 11 percent faster than non-ESOP companies, the underlying belief is that employees who are now part owners are more motivated.

Financial advisors play a vital role in the process, because in order for the seller to qualify for tax free status, they must reinvest the proceeds into what is called a qualifying 1042 transaction. Advisors that are expert in these securities are needed, and for example, UBS has a group that is one of the preeminent groups in the country. These securities are usually very long-term bonds with a forty-year or longer maturity issued by blue chip companies with excellent credit. They normally can be highly margined, meaning the seller of the company can get almost all the cash from the sale to use as they see fit.

ESOPs are very complicated, and experts like Don—a financial advisor well versed in ESOPs—as well as attorneys, are needed to implement these plans. However, if the seller's firm qualifies, these are exceptional programs that benefit the seller and the employees alike.

One would think that for the subset of investors who are business owners, that the vast majority would at least be aware that there are advisors who cater to small business owners—or be aware of tools like ESOPS—given the dramatic benefit they offer. However, for the reasons illustrated in future chapters, such beneficial offerings are largely unknown.

A NEED FOR INFORMATION AND EDUCATION

"When I think of financial advisors I think of someone that is not neutral and does not have my best interests at heart. I think there is an ulterior motive to sell a product from their company or some other company," Julie Miller stated. "Twenty years ago, I had an advisor, referred by a friend who thought they were good. It turned out they just wanted to sell us insurance products." Julie's feeling and experience is unfortunately not unique nor new.

During our phone conversation, Julie explained to me that, although she was a business major in college, she recalls only one class thirty years ago that discussed investing. In retrospect, she wishes that classes in investing and personal finance were more prevalent, as she is not clear if she is prepared for her financial future. Julie has always contributed the maximum to her 401k, as her company has a great match, but is unclear on how much she'll need for retirement. Or, for that matter, should she start thinking about long term care insurance? What other questions should she be asking herself? These are very important inquiries, especially since she is separated and preparing for divorce.

Julie has not made that many securities investments outside her 401k, but apparently has good instincts. When Tesla was trading at about twenty-eight or thirty dollars per share, her sense was that this company could be the next Ford

Motors, and she urged her husband to buy the stock. He reluctantly did, and within five years, the stock was at 185 dollars per share. However, without telling Julie, he put a sell stop on some of the shares, and as the stock had some erratic price movements, some of the stock was sold. As of this writing, the stock is just over three hundred dollars per share. Julie confided that she is not exactly sure how sell-stop orders work and wonders if her husband does either. They also purchased some Alibaba stock, which has performed well for them.

Julie has learned some valuable lessons through her experiences. First, she believes couples should be much more transparent with each other when it comes to money and their perceptions about money. She wishes she found a financial advisor they could have trusted in the past to help them better understand their money differences. She now sees the value of an advisor, but wishes she hired one years ago. Another realization is to not fully depend on a spouse and assume their level of financial understanding. For example, Julie's husband was in the banking industry, but he had knowledge gaps as well, which was a surprise to her. Additionally, she wishes she kept her pre-marital assets in her name only. Her attorneys believe she will be fine, but if she hadn't transferred things to joint name, it would have been easier.

As our conversation came to a close, Julie was very surprised to learn that there were many female advisors around the country that offered financial planning to divorcees as a niche client base. She was also excited to learn that many of these advisors just did financial plans and nothing else, which gave her some comfort, given she will be going through some significant changes in the near future.

BASIC FINANCIAL EDUCATION IS LACKING

In 2010, The Financial Literacy Group wrote the white paper "Barriers to Financial Advice for Non-Affluent Consumers," which was sponsored by the Society for Actuaries. This document pointed to a lack of basic financial education as a root cause of low advisor use by non-affluent consumers. The paper notes that consumers need a base level of education to feel comfortable searching for an advisor, and that lack of basic education prevents them from even looking for advice.

The paper quoted the 2007 Health and Retirement Study, which is sponsored by the National Institute on Aging, that showed half of all older workers did not even know what kind of retirement plan they had. Less than 20 percent of workers in the population knew the correct age at which they were eligible for Social Security benefits. The study cites many examples of low financial education levels as being one of the primary drivers to using a financial advisor.

I believe that it is an accurate assumption. If a consumer does not understand basic concepts—like how a stock and bond are different—then that consumer's ability to understand financial advisors and the various types is even less likely.

MANY INDUSTRY OBSERVERS ALSO LESS INFORMED

While writing this book, I have been asked by industry observers about various aspects of the financial advisor industry. I was asked by one well-known and experienced industry individual, "This kind of advisor is better than that kind, correct?"

The actual question asked was so basic that it was analogous to someone asking, "Advisors who wear blue suits are better than those that wear grey suits, correct?" I do not blame the person who asked the question. I think the organization that originally hired and trained him should have spent more time on his or her education. To be clear, this person does know something about advisors, but not enough to be a consumer influencer.

The main thrust of the question was single-mindedly focused on one attribute of advisors. In our long conversation, no questions were asked about how to gauge an advisor by their experience, services offered, investment style, types of clients, legal history, or any other attribute that should go into determining the proper fit for an investor to hire them. It was yet again a reminder that so many people from so many walks of life simply do not understand the basics of advisors.

BUT WHY ARE SO MANY UNINFORMED?

But the underlying question remains: why is the American public so uninformed about financial advisors? In the next four chapters, I will explain the four main drivers, which are important to understand so that you can better search and engage with an advisor. These four drivers inform our conscious and subconscious perception of financial advisors in general. Understanding why this vital professional group are misunderstood gives you the comfort to undertake your search or gain deeper understanding of your current advisor with a more open mind. Armed with the right questions, this will allow you to make a more informed search.

CHAPTER 8

HOW WALL STREET HAS MARRED THE PERCEPTION OF FINANCIAL ADVISORS

We can't rewrite history. But we can learn from it. Misperceptions about financial advisors became more widespread in the 1970s, when retail Wall Street began to create a multitude of financial products. In their wake, an aggressive sales culture was spawned to promote proprietary investments. This culture gave rise to firms that hired young, aggressive salespeople with tactics showcased in films like *Wall Street*, *Boiler Room*, and *The Wolf of Wall Street*. Exposes, investigations, and market corrections, all added to the misperceptions.

To set the record straight, at that time the percentage of advisors who were purely salespeople was much higher than it is today. In fact, in the 1970s and 1980s, there were very few financial advisors—less than a few thousand—and certainly even fewer that catered to the average investor. They were primarily brokers, and there was very little confusion due to nomenclature like today. For example, today there is tremendous confusion over the terms "broker" versus "financial advisor" titles. To be fair, the conduct in the 1970s and 1980s varied widely from being a pure salesperson relying upon on the suitability standard, all the way to acting as a fiduciary, despite not legally being required to do so.

"Wall Street" is a term everyone around the globe has heard and knows well. It is synonymous with wealth, power, success, and (to some) greed and improper actions. It is also a term that is jargon, meaning different things to different people, but generally most people think Wall Street when they think of anything to do with investing in stocks or bonds. The unfortunate actions of firms that are most closely affiliated with Wall Street, or are literally on Wall Street, has led to an undeserved tainting of financial advisors who genuinely help individual investors. What most people do not know is that the vast majority of advisors do not work for firms that are "Wall Street" firms. Even advisors that work for true Wall Street firms can often be wholly unrelated and unaffected day to day by the actions of the corporation that employs them.

Most people are aware that Wall Street is the actual name of a street in lower Manhattan, New York, where—for many years—a significant concentration of brokerage firms were headquartered. And of course, the New York Stock Exchange is on Wall Street, at the corner of Wall Street and Broad Street. Wall Street is an east-west street running from Broadway all the way to the East River. It is called Wall Street as there was once a literal seven-foot-high wood wall there to keep the American Indians out of the early Dutch settlement, which originally occupied the area. As the most famous area of the New York financial district, Wall Street is full of rich history in its buildings, landmarks, and stories of historic figures like JP Morgan, Alexander Hamilton, and countless others.

I started my career working at 14 Wall Street in the mid-1980s, at then-Shearson Lehman Hutton, now Morgan Stanley. Next I worked at Waterhouse Securities, now TD Ameritrade at 44 Wall Street, which later moved to 100 Wall Street. I have a great deal of respect, admiration, awe, and fascination for the history across hundreds of years of the people and firms that operated on Wall Street. However, the scandals, greed, and hubris that is also part of that history has had a horrible effect on the perception of the advisors who serve individual investors. I hope this chapter will help separate these largely corporate scandals from the individual advisors who serve the individual investor, and help you understand that this negative history is a contributing factor to the hesitancy a large percentage of consumers have towards financial advisors.

To be very fair to history, from the 1970s through the early 1990s, the percentage of bad acting brokers and advisors that focused on retail investors was much higher than it is today; therefore, the negative perception of advisors is not solely due to corporate scandals that made headlines. However, the retail advice business has cleaned up to a very large degree relative to where it was, but the perception is still stuck many years behind the new reality. It bears repeating that every industry has its bad apples, and the financial advice business is no different. Unfortunately, however, its current image does not reflect the current reality.

WE JUST DO NOT KNOW ANY BETTER

So why does Wall Street at large share some of the burden of the unfair negative perception of financial advisors? To begin with, it's the lack of basic understanding of how retail advice operates by consumers. I mentioned above that the vast majority of financial advisors do not work for Wall Street firms. There is a subset called independent broker dealers and Registered Investment Advisers that employ over four hundred thousand financial advisors, versus the approximately fifty thousand advisors employed by the large four Wall Street firms. The four hundred thousand work for firms that you have never heard of—small, local advisory firms that have simple business models. Yet, when a Wall Street giant runs afoul of the law and it receives headlines for days, human nature in the absence of this market knowledge applies the negative connotation to *all* firms, big or small.

COMPLEXITY AND SIZE

Another reason Wall Street at large harms the advisor perception is that firms that are so large and complex are bound to get bad headlines when something goes wrong. When a large brokerage firm is a Registered Investment Adviser, a bank, an insurance company, and also brings companies public—not to mention, does ten other things as conglomerates do—when things go bad, headlines will be bad and there goes the perception again. When the brand of the conglomerate is synonymous with retail advice and other financial services offering bad public relations, it harms all participants at some level.

NOTABLE FRAUDS

Almost everyone reading this has heard of the Bernard Madoff Ponzi scheme. He has become a household word. Movies have been made, books written, and Madoff holds the world record for the largest Ponzi scheme at sixty-five billion dollars.

Have you ever heard of Nicholas Cosmo? Likely not, but he was dubbed the "Mini-Madoff" as his Ponzi scheme was found out one year after Madoff. His fraud was four hundred million dollars, and by some accounts, much worse than Madoff...as Cosmo's victims were almost completely middle-class, whose loss of twenty-five thousand dollars, for example, was their entire savings. Madoff mostly swindled high net worth investors. Madoff by contrast was a Wall Street titan by all accounts and was so for over twenty years.

One of the main reasons Madoff's fraud was so devasting to everyday financial advisors was that the Madoff story dominated the press for so long, and the ripple effect harmed all advisors. One of the reasons why Madoff dominated the press for so long was his record-breaking size of fraud, but a big part of why the press was so focused on Madoff was because he was viewed as a genuine institution by everyone on Wall Street, well-known for his market-making securities business. It is a nearly literal statement to say that every firm on Wall Street had a contract and worked with Madoff Securities. He was a past CEO of NASDAQ, the very first electronic stock exchange. He was a proverbial pillar of Wall Street society. The realization and shock that someone that ingrained into the fabric of the street being an outright criminal was just not fathomable at the time. It therefore stayed in the news cycle for far longer than, say, if he had been some much lesser-known financial predator like Cosmo.

Madoff ran what appeared to be a very legitimate NASDAQ Market Maker, which was conceptually a competing Wall Street firm to the New York Stock Exchange Specialists that once proliferated the floor of the Exchange. When I worked at the advisor division of Waterhouse Securities, our firm, like so many others, used Madoff Securities to execute trades. I went to their offices in Jersey City and met some of the staff. It was not until after he was jailed that research suggested the unit everyone used never made money and was, in fact, financially propped up by his Ponzi scheme division—the Registered Investment Adviser unit.

I personally was never even aware that Madaff managed money, and a lot of others I know were not aware that he managed money either. Of course, there were doubters of Madoff; Harry Markopolos was the most famous, as he was ignored by the SEC for years. This all contributed to the shock of the fraud, and that made the news rippled to advisors, and still does to this day. "Madoff-Proofing" is a word some use now when evaluating an advisor.

There are other notable scandals, such as the LIBOR rate fixing, the "London Whale" trader at JP Morgan, insider trading schemes—including the Martha Stewart prison sentence—and of course, the biggest one of all, which many Americans consider the housing and financial crisis of 2008.

PROPRIETARY PRODUCTS

Wall Street firms create their own investments called proprietary products. They can be mutual funds, insurance products, banking products, alternative, and others. By themselves, there is nothing wrong with a large financial conglomerate creating an innovative new financial product that taps into an opportunity or solves a particular problem. However, there have been two major types of abuses that have grabbed news headlines and, because of bad conduct on the part of a small minority, have tarnished the image of the broader spectrum of financial advisors.

First, over the course of time, there have been investment products created that either should never have been created, or their utility was for such a narrow universe of investors that any harm they created would not have gotten to the national stage. Bad proprietary investment products have been an issue for a long time, but in fairness, the issue has been a declining one over the past twenty years. The stigma, however, has not diminished.

I witnessed this first hand in my first year at Shearson Lehman Hutton, right out of college. I am not aware of any scandals per se from the products created that year, but I lived through the experience first-hand and experienced how investors often reacted negatively. In one calendar year, the firm created nine closed-end bond funds. Closed-end funds trade on an exchange, like the New York Stock Exchange, or NASDAQ, unlike open-ended funds, which do not. When this firm created a new investment product, the management pushed the brokers hard to sell that fund. There was normally a lot of pressure to sell these investments. Being right out of college, I asked some of the older brokers there what they thought of these securities. In essence, the older brokers said to me, "Hey kid, smarten up! How can any firm really create nine new bond funds in one year that all serve a unique utility?" So, I did some deeper research into one particular fund. It was a fund that provided an interest rate that was essentially the same interest rate as every other bond fund. The fund invested in a mix of U.S. and Canadian bonds. The added value, and the reason for investing in the fund, was that if the Canadian dollar and the American dollar ever moved away from each other in value, this fund would generate additional income far above the guaranteed rate. Here is the problem: in the fifty years prior, the U.S. and the Canadian dollar never deviated from each other much at all.

So, I went back to the older brokers I was speaking with and told them this, and asked again, why would the firm create this investment knowing full well this investment will almost assuredly do no better than any other, like security? They said simply that the fees the firm would earn from creating such a product would be in the millions, and that's why they pumped out nine in one year. Most of those funds were not unique—no one got hurt from my understanding, but there was no true purpose for them to the investor over other similar investments that were available. You may be familiar with other products that actually did create harm and got lots of negative press, such as Collateral Debt Obligations (CDOs), Auction Rate Securities (ARS), and many others. CDOs were one of the leading causes of the financial crisis of 2008.

The second major issue around proprietary products was the occasional and extraordinary sales pressure applied to sell these things. The pressure was applied in many ways back then, from your manager simply stating to your face, "you must sell fifty thousand dollars of this new security," to incentives and gifts, like lobsters flown in from Maine gifted to the top three sellers in the branch, to the financial incentive of the firm paying a higher commission rate if you sold proprietary products.

Thankfully, over the years pressure tactics from management have been made largely illegal, and these types of incentives to push a product are much less frequent today. However, the damage of the high-pressure sales tactics forced on the broker, who then often pressured clients, and prospects has taken its toll via bad word of mouth and negative publicity. There continue to be, and likely will always be, some percentage of poor conduct that mars the image of advisors. The recent scandals of JP Morgan's purported mutual fund sales abuses, and more recently, Wells Fargo abuses of false new bank accounts, are two examples of scandals that make it harder for quality advisors to do their work.

REAL AND PERCEIVED CONFLICTS OF INTEREST

Advisors who work for the large, household name firms get national attention when they violate rules, regulations, and laws. These firms and their advisor-employees have more real and perceived conflicts of interest than firms that are smaller, regional, or local. Please note that I write *more* conflicts of interest. Every advisor, like every human being on this planet, has a conflict of interest. The real question to ask is—what are those conflicts? Is the potential for that conflict so big that I don't want to work with you, or is it just fine? Large Wall Street firms have multiple divisions, product lines, and essentially, many things to sell. They are regulated by as many as six different regulators. They are very complex firms, and on top of that, they are publicly held...so the pressure to increase profitability is significant.

Because of all their complexity, any conflicts within these firms have become issues for their retail clients. There are fines and penalties levied when their advisors sometimes recommend a product that turns out to be the wrong product. There are violations that occur when they provide an investment that pays a higher commission, when a very similar product that costs the investor less is available. There is theft, fraud, and outright poor advice. These kinds of transgressions are actually perpetrated by advisors at all types of firms, but because of the sheer size and notoriety, their problems affect the good advisors at those same firms, and other firms and are magnified in the mind of investors.

As I explain in other chapters of this book, the percentage of all advisors that run afoul of their regulations is actually lower than the percentage of doctors and lawyers that run afoul of their regulations. Financial instutitions just receive so much more bad press.

ACCOUNT MINIMUMS

An unwitting culprit in the misinformation of consumers and investors is the fact that Wall Street advisory/brokerage firms have had high investment minimums for years, and those minimums have increased with time. The increasing minimums get national press, as do most changes at these large firms. When you read these articles, you almost never read about competing firms that outnumber the large firms by advisor headcount by three to one and don't have any minimums! In this case, the media has some blame in the misinformation process, by not fully reporting the landscape. In the absence of other facts, consumers and investors for decades have been programmed to believe that they are not rich enough for an advisor.

However, in recent years, as market forces and the Robo-Advisor movement took shape, these large Wall Street firms have all created units to cater to smaller accounts, and have even created their own Robo-Advisor platforms. This is a good and smart change, but it is late coming, and the imprint of decades of a consistent the high-minimum message has done its damage. It will likely take years for Wall Street firms to undo that negative impression.

SEPARATING WALL STREET FROM ADVISORS

It is important to reiterate that the misdeeds of Wall Street firms should not automatically be conferred onto any financial advisor, whether they be employed directly by a Wall Street firm, or some small, local advisor halfway across the country. The corporate decisions and corporate actions are separate from the daily work that advisors perform. It is true, however, that some advisors do and will follow corporate pressure, as it applies to those that work for Wall Street firms. However, those numbers are dwindling; in fact, there have always been advisors who essentially ignored and were immune to corporate pressure. To be fair, these do tend to be the older advisors from larger firms. I saw this first hand at the 14 Wall Street office when I was a rookie. The older brokers rarely sold these redundant manufactured offerings, they were never recipients of prize contests like trips or lobsters, and remember this was back in the mid- to late-1980s when the management pressure was dramatically higher, and the compliance oversight was much less. Even in those days, many veteran brokers I saw did what they felt was best for their clients.

CHAPTER 9

THE FINANCIAL SERVICES INDUSTRY CONFUSES

The financial services industry has to take some of the heat. The problem is that they've done a poor job of explaining themselves.

The retail financial services industry is complicated and intangible and it's not an exact science. A pressing problem is that there isn't a singular, powerful trade association representing the financial advisor niche. Instead, there are more than forty trade associations, each insisting that it's the "leading" industry voice. Making matters worse, many financial services companies go to great lengths to bash their competition. The result: Needless, self-destructive infighting, confusion, misinformation, and reinforcement of prevailing myths. If the industry cannot get its act together, how can it educate the public, and eliminate—or at least reduce—negative misperceptions?

MILK AND BEEF AND DIAMONDS

These taglines are likely memorable to you: "A Diamond is Forever," "Beef, It's What's for Dinner," and "Got Milk"? The diamond, beef, and milk industries thought that it was wise to conduct long-term ad campaigns to educate the public about the virtues of their products. It worked, and consumption of those products continued to increase for many years. Advertising does indeed work, and that is why firms and associations do it. Most industries have one trade association, perhaps two, that promote the virtues of their offerings. It is a very old concept; it works and creates demand for that product or service. Trade advertising also allows an entire industry to educate on single topics, lobby and communicate trends, which can have a very beneficial effect—especially when an industry is going through rapid change or is threatened by shifts in the ecosystem.

Do you recall that famous financial advice tagline? Me neither...because one does not exist. Financial services are one of the odd industries where there is no overarching trade association that exists for the greater good of all competing members. However, the reality is much worse. Not only is there no one overarching theme or message that the entire industry gets behind, but there are literally dozens of trade groups that encompass insurance, brokerage, and advice, all with their own messages.

There are competing groups in financial services that are centered around the type of security they are promoting, around the type of firm an advisor works for, how a person is paid, and informed by the business model the firms operate under. Many do not have consumer-facing marketing budgets, but some do. There are even regulators that, from the outside looking in, appear to compete with each other. For certain, these regulators do not cooperate effectively.

If there was one organization they all belonged to that espoused "Financial Guidance" or some other moniker, advertised consistently, this would go far to turning popular perception to where it naturally should be.

INFIGHTING AND SELF HATE

A troubling trend is the disproportionate amount of writing in the advisor trade press on the internal strife the industry has between competing types of firms, as well as a focus on the small number of advisors that run afoul of the law. The collective negativity has an effect, and likely spills over in advisors' communication with everyday consumers and investors.

BAD ACTORS

Bad conduct from that small number of advisors is obviously horrible public relations. While every industry will always have some unscrupulous persons in the industry, the financial advisor industry has a lot of ground to make up to help correct a public perception that is very unbalanced. One of the ways to do this is self-expunge the bad actors. Elsewhere in the book, I estimate that about 3 percent of advisors have negative history so bad that they should be permanently barred from the industry. These are advisors, and most often, they are in reality salespeople and not true advice givers, who have been fired from five, ten, even fifteen firms in a twenty-year career. These are people that have twenty, thirty, or more items that are disclosed on their regulatory history. Fines, reconstitution of lost moneys, disciplinary actions, misdemeanors, and even felonies, appear on the public record of these people. The problem is that the firms that employ these bad actors make money from these advisors and they don't want to lose the revenue. If the industry on its own got together to remove these people and publicized that fact, perception and trust would increase. My guess is that if this action was communicated well and often, public perception could actually lift significantly and quickly.

BASHING THE COMPETITION

There is a growing number of advisors who bash their competition, and mostly in subtle ways. I know this first hand, because over the last year, I have personally helped friends and family find advisors and have reached out to advisors to create a short list for them to consider. Very often, the advisor will say something like, "What I stand for is this or that, and this is important because not everyone else does...." The problem with this mentality is that consumers can tell you are bashing your competition, and most people really dislike it. This becomes more and more true as you get increasingly sophisticated investors. Most sales professionals have been taught that negative selling does not work. Customers do not want to be in the middle of advisors' turf battle, and speaking negatively of anything is, well...negative. Consumers of anything want the experience to be happy and uplifting. I believe the reason there is competitor bashing is because there is less and less professional sales training being conducted at firms, and if the firm is small, zero sales training. Sales is taught as an undergraduate degree at dozens of universities around the country, so sales per se is not a bad thing. Some advisors oddly believe it is, and don't consider themselves as selling anything, especially when there are incoming leads. The collective negativity drags down the perception of the entire industry. There are more than enough ways for an advisor to positively differentiate themselves than to go negative.

POOR MARKETING

Historically, financial advisors were never well marketed, if indeed any marketing was done at all. Most advisors built their businesses by personal direct selling, but that has gotten harder and stifled by changes in regulation and compliance. The lack of marketing is a problem; for example, small advisory businesses or financial planning businesses literally do no advertising, and there are a great many people that are unaware they exit. The odd thing is that most advisory firms have grown by referral via friends, family, or professional networking, and if you survived, you kept on growing. Bull markets certainly helped the growth. Most advisors have been very happy with their rates of growth, yet oddly, so many people are unaware of their existence or lack a clear understanding of their value.

To reiterate, in the absence of a contra-narrative, the prevailing narrative is what people will believe. No marketing by the majority of small advisors means a lot of Americans think advisors are either not necessary, not competent, or a Madoff. Paradoxically, there is a contingent of advisors who fear growth, because they don't want to manage a "business"; they want to perform their craft and keep making their comfortable living. In this scenario the consumers who need the help, but are unaware of the advisors that can help them, are the ones who lose.

Unfortunately, much of the marketing done by advisors isn't of high quality. I cannot tell you how many advisor websites have a compass on the home page with some type of "we will chart your course for your financial future" or a "we offer objective wealth management" type statement. Most people won't have an idea either statement means. Consequently, the reader doesn't learn anything and probably will continue what they're doing now...which for many, is nothing.

The good news is that in the last few years, many more advisors have realized that better marketing across all tactical aspects, such as social, website, content, and outbound, are now essential. This started after the recession of 2008, when advisors literally lost clients through no fault of their own—rather, the market correction forced advisors to realize that they must communicate their value much better than they had been previously. In the ensuing years, more service providers were created, and regulators and the firms finally accepted common social media usage. Starting in 2015, there has been a renaissance of financial technology firms created to solve very specific financial problems, and many of these companies are pure marketing oriented or have features that are associated to marketing. All this bodes well for better communication going forward.

JARGON

This industry is highly technical and often filled with jargon. The problem is that many advisors believe that throwing around jargon makes them appear intelligent and expert. What they fail to realize is jargon does not communicate to consumers—it alienates them. In some cases, the consumer may feel stupid, which is a negative experience, and that pushes people away. In most cases, they simply do not know what they are reading. The reader does not get informed, or gets irritated and moves on. Imagine if you read a website, marketing literature, or heard a speech, and 50 percent of the words were in a language you didn't speak.

You not only would fail to understand what was trying to be communicated, you likely would get frustrated. This is an absurd example, but it proves the point that when advisors use terms that are not understood by all, then statistically, you are failing to communicate to a percentage of your audience. Jargon is just another reason why the financial industry has a problem communicating their true value to investors and consumers.

PRODUCT PUSHING

When an advisor focuses on one investment product, be it a mutual fund, stock, insurance policy, or private partnership, to provide or sell you, they are "pushing a product." In its worst form, the advisor calls you, or leads the conversation by discussing a very specific product, or worse yet, has a complicated long presentation that solves a problem, and the solution to that problem by no coincidence happens to be their preferred product. Almost always they get compensated in one way, shape, or form. This practice was very commonplace in the 1960s through the 1980s. In the 1990s the practice started to drop dramatically through a combination of regulatory reform, enforcement actions against bad actors, and competitive forces. However, it is still done today, and likely will continue forever, albeit in the future it will likely be in very isolated circumstances. I discuss in other chapters how to quickly spot and avoid these people.

To take a big step back, there is nothing wrong with selling a product. If you think about commerce in general, most of us work for companies that at some level in the organization, an employee must sell a product or service. The saying "Nothing happens until someone sells something," has been attributed to Henry Ford, Mary Kay Ash, Sam Walton, Peter Drucker, and other business and thought leaders. There is a right way to sell and a wrong way, and therein lies the key to being professional and completely honest in your sales, ultimately benefitting the investor.

The correct way to sell to an investor is to adopt business to business sales practices. When I left being a retail stockbroker and went into the business to business side of the financial advisory business in 1991, I studied and took coursework to learn how to sell to businesses. The essential theme is that if you identify that your prospect has a problem, and if your product or products can solve that problem, then you have the ability to make a sale. From there, if your product or service is the best for your prospect, then—and only then—should you make a sale. I used to give this example to junior sales people I trained. Imagine if you are a sales executive working for GE selling jet engines. One of your prospects is

Boeing and they are building a new jet. If you attempted to hard sell them your engine that was the wrong fit for that plane, people would die. In business to business sales, rarely do these sales professionals attempt the hard sell, high pressure sales techniques that we encounter in retail sales. It is just not done because of the ripple effect and ramifications if things go wrong.

In practice, here is the very short version of how it feels to be sold to professionally and ethically as a consumer/investor: the advisor asks lots of questions of you. The advisor takes lots of notes and asks follow-up questions to your answers. The advisor invites you to ask any and all questions of him or her. The advisor answers them all fully, and if they cannot give you an immediate answer, they get back to you with the answer. At the conclusion, the advisor may say you should work together, but perhaps not. A specific product is normally not part of the conversation. I have many more details on this in later chapters.

Anyone who is still a product pusher is harming the entire financial advice industry, because human nature is to tell ten times more people about a negative experience than a positive one, so the narrative gets to be outsized. This current practice by some, coupled with the actual history of high rates of product pushing, is yet another reason why the perception of advisors is more negative than it should be.

RETURNING PHONE CALLS

This might seem like an odd thing to write, but the reality is that many advisors are not as responsive as they should be, and this does not help reinforce the great work they do. This has been not only written about in trade journals, but in report after report on why investors fire their advisor, responsiveness is usually top of the list. For example, in a recent Spectrem Group, Millionaire Corner survey, "slow to return phone calls" was the number one reason why investors fired their advisors. I also have very recent personal experience to reinforce these reports.

As I have said, I've helped family members and friends find advisors over the past year or so. In each case I searched, selected, and called several advisors to create a short list of advisors for my friends to select from. I spoke with the advisor first to make sure they were interested in my friend and/or family member.

Invariably, I did not get the advisor on the phone when I called and had to leave a message with either someone who answered the phone, or on the voice-mail system. Most of the time I did not get a call back for one, two, or even three days. From a pure sales or customer service perspective, this is not what I as the consumer want to experience. It leaves a bad impression. It makes me think the advisor is not too interested in taking new clients or they are bad business people.

TRANSITIONING FROM A PRACTICE TO A BUSINESS

There is a macro-reason why some of the issues in this chapter exist, and that is the broader financial advice business is going through a transformation at the individual advice giver level. The vast majority of advisory groups are owned or led by a person who still gives advice to individual clients. The transformation is that these people have always perceived themselves as a practitioner of financial advice, and—much like attorneys, CPAs, or doctors—are practitioners of their craft; however, they now realize they must treat their practices as businesses in order to grow, serve more clients, and improve what they do.

Professionals in the law, medical, and accounting fields have largely gone through these transformations ten to twenty years ago, and now financial advisors are going through theirs. This is an active transition as we speak and maintain basic business conduct that nearly every other business person adopts, such as returning calls quickly, having a top-notch website, encouraging sales training, and having a professional manager run their business. These are tasks that seem new and unique to many financial advisors. Advisors at large know they need to go through this transition, but many people and firms are at different phases of this change. It is an emotional and uncomfortable change for many.

AGING OF THE ADVISOR POPULATION

The majority of financial advisors are closer to retirement age, and as of today, not enough younger people are coming into the industry. We need the next generation to not only take the place of these older advisors, but to serve the growing number of Americans that need financial advice. If you know of a younger person who is unsure of what career to consider, suggest financial advice. A person that likes to help others and is detail-oriented will find the financial advice industry an emotionally rewarding career that will provide them with the economic benefit to support themselves and their families.

Messages that consumers hear or read from most of today's advisors does reflect the age gap and further creates a barrier in communicating the true value an advisor provides. The fact is, there have always been advisors that cater to young consumer and investors, albeit in much smaller numbers; however, when the marketing from most of the advice business comes from an older generation, the younger set don't get communicated to. The number of advisors serving younger investors is growing, but the gap is considerable.

HIDING IN PLAIN SIGHT

Depending on which report you believe, between 35–50 percent of Americans have a financial advisor. Also, according to most research papers, most of the clients of advisors are pleased with their advisor. According the U.S. census bureau in 2017, there were one hundred and twenty-six million households. Using the 35 percent number, that would mean forty-four million families have an advisor, with most of them happy with their advisor. With that many happy clients, one would think that word would spread very fast about getting an advisor...but clearly this has not happened. Why? The answer is that investors that currently have an advisor do not fully understand what their advisor does, and therefore, cannot share with confidence the benefit of having an advisor.

But why can't, or why won't, investors recommend their advisor to others? Part of the answer is that money and personal finances are deeply personal and many people do not bring these things up in conversation, as it's regarded in American culture as crass. Additionally, consumers often do not want to admit they need help or don't understand certain topics.

Another reason is because the advisor does not fully educate their client regarding simple language surrounding the financial industry. I have heard this from both investors and advisors alike. But the responsibility is the advisor's to fully explain what they do for a client, what goes into it, and what the ultimate benefit is. The trick is to do it in plain English in such a way that the investor can easily repeat it to other consumers or investors. Of course, having the investor so pleased with the outcome of their advisor's services and ultimately recommend them to others is the ideal goal.

The bottom line is that the financial advisor market does a very poor job of explaining to their own clients what they do, how they do it, and why it's beneficial. It's sad that many millions of consumers could be amazing emissaries of great advice givers and could theoretically spread the word to their neighbors and personal networks, solving personal finance problems for large swaths of the populace. To be fair to advisors, it is not simple to be able to explain and demonstrate the benefits of a complex intangible to a non-industry person. But the need is there.

Part of the difficulty is that financial advice in any form always touches upon how much money a person has or does not have. Even a flat-fee financial plan for a person that does not yet have stock investments, helping budget expenses and reducing debt as the primary task at hand, is hard to explain. It's not that the process is so tough to explain, it's that the person does not naturally want to share that they don't yet have a portfolio.

At the other side of the spectrum, families with wealth most often do not want to flaunt it and won't share their portfolio details with others. Speaking in generalities about financial advice without saying the actual dollar amount is not a natural progression in a conversation.

Until the financial advice industry can both explain their service plainly and teach their clients how to spread the word in a comfortable way, millions of satisfied advisor clients will be largely silent and not share their experience. This helps to explain the current narrative.

CHAPTER 10

REGULATORS MISS THE MARK

The financial services industry is regulated in an inefficient and unorganized way, and as a result, consumers both remain confused and exposed to fraud; meanwhile, those advisors and institutions are mistreated. For the consumer, there are two results of this poor system. One, if you are a victim of a major fraud such as the Madoff scheme, very often that fraud could have been stopped long ago and many would not have fallen victims. Two, the image of the majority of advisors is tarnished unfairly when regulators miss a Madoff. This means consumers don't get the help they need because they are miseducated or fearful.

I use the Madoff example as an easy story everyone can relate to, however, there are many types of bad conduct demonstrated by that small percentage of advisors who go missed for years or even decades. They include improper sales practices, outright theft, literally selling the incorrect investment product to an investor, advice being given by unlicensed persons, insider trading, Ponzi schemes, and more. There's a long list of improper behavior that harms investors.

The regulatory system is inept. Many that are employed by regulators have never worked in the industry. It's no surprise that they don't understand how the industry works. The pathetic result: Regulators concentrate on the wrong issues and fail to deal with pressing problems that need to be addressed. Is it any wonder that the majority of regulators have failed us? I've met regulators who lamented (off the record) that they were told by their supervisors to not waste time on petty frauds or unethical, unscrupulous advisors. The politics are reprehensible. I spent seven years working for a regulatory compliance consulting firm. As an insider, I learned that the regulators, Financial Industry Regulatory Authority (FINRA), Securities and Exchange Commission (SEC), and the state of New York, missed the Madoff Ponzi scheme, which had been going on for some time.

It's almost unfathomable that one of the biggest cases of financial fraud slipped right through their fingers. Do you think this massive screw-up by supposedly smart people tarnished financial advisors image? (Rhetorical question.)

The financial services industry must be regulated; however, it must be regulated in an effective manner. Today's regulatory oversight of the financial services industry is poorly constructed, poorly executed, and both consumers and those regulated suffer because of it. Here is a quick overview of how the financial services industry is regulated:

1. The Securities and Exchange Commission (SEC), a government division reporting to Congress regulates Registered Investment Advisers (RIA) if they have over one hundred million dollars in client assets.

2. Each state regulates RIAs for those firms that have under one hundred million dollars in client assets.

3. Most states, but not all, license the people that work for RIAs. The SEC does not.

4. The Financial Industry Regulatory Authority is not a government body, rather it is a Self-Regulatory Organization that governs broker-dealers, who in turn employ financial advisors (Registered Representatives is the technical term). It reports to the SEC but acts autonomously. It is funded by the firms it regulates.

5. Each state regulates insurance activity and oversees insurance companies, agencies, and agents. There is no national regulator, like the SEC or FINRA.

If the above appears to be confusing, it is. There are thousands of firms that are regulated by three different regulators: SEC, FINRA, and the State Insurance Commissioner. There are many tens of thousands of advisors who work for these firms that have to comply with three different sets of rules. For these firms it is not uncommon to get visited by three different regulators in the very same year. If the firm is larger, then add in a visit by other regulators from the banking world and the commodity world.

The Madoff scam was the crowning example of a poorly run system. The SEC and FINRA both had jurisdiction over Madoff, yet each agency initially blamed the other for missing the Madoff fraud. According to the 2009 SEC Office of Inspector General report, had the SEC gone directly to the DTC, which is essentially the financial institution every brokerage firm uses to hold stocks, to verify his statements, instead of just getting a copy from Madoff—fake documents, we later found out—the SEC would have caught Madoff in 1992, not in 2008 when he confessed.

Fraud and corruption expert L. Burke Files responded to this same Madoff and DTC question on Quora on February 6, 2016, explaining:

"The SEC has hired mostly attorneys and accountants—not people saturated in the deeds and mis-deeds of the markets. The SEC needs to find those retired backroom officers and due diligence professionals to understand where else to look for information. They need people saturated in the deeds of the market—not just attorneys and accountants—and with these people, to build teams of investigators with broader skills and experience. To their defense—sure enough I have seen advertisements from the SEC looking for just such people."

To my mind, running an ad is simply not enough. The heads of the various regulatory bodies need to aggressively seek out the best minds and experienced people on Wall Street to actually find the fraud early on and stop it before it balloons. That means hiring retained search firms to find the best and the brightest and recruit from the Goldman Sachs, Morgan Stanleys, and Merrills of the world. That would also mean paying top dollar, but that investment would stop the frauds much earlier, and also create regulation that makes practical sense. In the long run, the savings would be significant.

NEW YORK STATE OF MIND

There are many examples of inconsistent rules, regulations, and laws that make the regulatory system a mess, and eventually, a problem for investors. New York is one of a few states that do not require people that give advice on behalf of Registered Investment Advisers (RIA) to register with the state and identify themselves. They are invisible! What this means is, if you want to do some background research on the person that is an RIA and you decide to use the SEC or FINRA site—where most other RIAs and broker-dealer Registered Reps are disclosed—you will not find them!

This is unbelievable, as the second largest state in the union, the home base of the largest Ponzi Scheme in history (Madoff), would not be interested in knowing who is giving advice. They do, however, need to take an exam to give advice, but all these advice givers are literally nowhere to be found in a regulator's database to know if they even took an exam!

After I re-read the State of New York requirements in March of 2018, I decided to check with advisors I knew who worked for large, very reputable RIA firms in NY. The advisors either were simply not in the database, or worse, the system would read "This person is no longer registered as of December 2014," as one example. That makes this RIA firm look like they are a law breaker by employing someone who is not registered, because the regulator sites do not share that a few states don't register. It is incredibly sloppy and inconsistent.

Now, I get the whole states' rights issue. States and the federal government have their controls, checks, and balances put forth at the founding of this country. But your average consumer could not care less that New York is exercising its right to govern its businesses as seen fit. They care about making sure their advisor is not a crook, and common sense would dictate that all regulators put together a system that covers everyone, to make it easy for the consumer to use, avoiding fraud while instilling confidence.

REGULATORS WILL VISIT YOUR DOOR...OR NOT

FINRA physically visits as many as 50 percent of all the nation's close to four thousand broker-dealers each year. The SEC, however, has audited via live examination just 11 percent or less from 2012–2016 of the advisors it regulates. In fact, according to the SEC, 35 percent of RIAs have never been physically examined. The individual state RIA examination data is not available in consolidated form, but—for example—during 2014–2017, an average of less than 10 percent of the California RIAs were physically examined.

Here is the question: given that broker-dealers, SEC RIAs, and State RIAs often provide the same service to investors, why are some visited frequently and some rarely? Broker-dealers can offer extremely complicated services with far more conflicts of interest to be sure. However, many are fairly simple in the services they offer investors. The disparity in physical visits—or exams, as they are called—makes no common sense. Moreover, a full one-third of SEC RIAs have never been visited. At some point, one must adopt a big picture view and simply state that this structure is just begging for problems. That is one of the reasons to this day we still see frauds and Ponzi schemes that otherwise could have been stopped much earlier.

Every time a fraud is prosecuted later than otherwise possible, consumers get more jaded and hesitant to find the advice they need. You rarely hear that a person is dubious as to the value of a doctor, as greater society has come to the conclusion that seeing a doctor is smart for your health. If the majority of society would come to the collective conclusion that getting financial advice is smart for their financial health, there would be so many more lives improved. This metaphor transcends money, considering additional resources would be applied to things like education and health care.

CONGRESS'S IMPACT ON THE FINANCIAL SERVICES INDUSTRY

Congress influences the financial services industry in significant ways. For example, it approves the annual SEC budget, which among other things, includes the funding of examiners to inspect Registered Investment Advisers. Congress closely scrutinizes financial advisory firms, and regularly holds hearings to expose wrongdoing.

To protect the public, Congress applies intense pressure on the SEC and other governmental bodies. But the public seldom reads about Congressional hearings investigating wrongdoing by either medical or legal professionals. Any pressure on these professionals is minimal at best.

The SEC lives in a somewhat psychotic environment. In 2017, it appeared the SEC made hundreds of millions in "profit" from securities filing fees, penalties, and related revenue. But Congress does not allow the commission to keep it. The SEC must argue for the money back every year via a budgeting process. This has been reported by others in years past and is not news. What is frustrating for the industry is that the very Congress that takes away money from the SEC simultaneously criticizes it for not examining enough advisory firms. It can be likened to a Monty Python episode about absurdity. Supposedly, Congress does not allow the SEC to keep the money it earns because Congress doesn't want the SEC to levy fines and over-regulate, just to bloat some SEC bureaucrat's fiefdom. If it were up to me, I'd rather have more scrutiny than less in a post-Madoff world. The SEC can't pay the best and brightest to ferret out genius madmen like Madoff. But if the SEC is self-funded, why not try giving them their money back for a few years? The results could be surprising.

The folks who work at the SEC extend their frustration to those they regulate. There is scrutiny and the pressure to innovate and change, but we remain without the essential resources and tools to find the bad guys, or the budget necessary to hire qualified staff and obtain the technology and tools to make it happen. It's all smoke and mirrors. Or, to adapt part of a timeless quote from Shakespeare's *Macbeth*, the SEC's polished doublespeak is "full of sound and fury, signifying nothing."

MY LUNCH WITH BARRY

This story you have likely read, heard, and seen before; however, it really happened to me and is sadly common. "Barry" is the name I'm giving to a regulator I had lunch with six years ago. Barry works for one of the regulators I mention above. I will not even share which specific regulator, as I do not want to run any risk of Barry being subject to retribution from his superiors.

Barry is a twenty-year veteran regulator, an attorney, and a good friend of a former work colleague. At the time I was conducting interviews for a newly created position at my company for the General Counsel position. Barry had terrific credentials and I had great respect for my colleague, so I proceeded to interview him for the position. Over the course of our lunch, I asked him why he wanted to leave his job as a regulator. One of the primary reasons for him to consider leaving was he was directly instructed by his superiors to not pursue prosecution of smaller frauds. It was incredibly frustrating for him to know that in a small town, twenty, thirty, and forty people were literally robbed by a fraudster who stole their modest life savings and his boss told him not to pursue it. The reason not to pursue it was his boss wanted him to both focus on larger frauds, and frauds where their odds of winning would be higher. In short, if there was a chance of professional embarrassment and the crook was small, move on.

For most of you, this story is familiar as it's been told in the context of police stories, legal stories and whistleblower sagas either coming from real life or fictionalized accounts. However, if you put yourself in the victim's shoes and you've been taken for fifty thousand or seventy-five thousand dollars and the regulator overseeing this crime refuses to pursue it, how would you feel? At that lunch I was very angry as I heard this story, but Barry said it was commonplace, as most regulators are highly political. The practice of not prosecuting every crime has multiple ill effects. The current victims are obviously harmed, but so are future victims. When the public learns of such a practice, public faith in regulators is diminished. These are additive reasons for massive misperceptions of advisors and the entire industry.

FOR THE NEXT TEN YEARS TELL EVERYONE YOU BROKE THE LAW

In 2014 I had a client in Pennsylvania who was both an RIA and a broker representative for an Independent Broker Dealer. Due to the nature of the marketing and public relations software application my firm provided to him, we needed to review any public disclosures he had on record. He had been in the business for fifteen years and did financial planning along with investment management. His broker record had no disclosures, but his RIA record had one disclosure, resulting from an on-site visit the regulator made to his office. This is from memory, but it stuck out, and it read something like: "This advisor has violated a Pennsylvania State rule and as the penalty, must disclose on the Form ADV for a period of ten years that the advisor violated said rule." This was a scary statement on this advisor's record, and I wondered what exactly the guy did. Also, what is very important to know is that the Form ADV is a document that an RIA must offer to provide to his clients every single year. He also, by law, must provide the ADV to each potential client he meets. So, for the next ten years, this advisor must advertise to his clients and prospects alike that he violated a state law! Mind you, years prior, I spent six years working at National Regulatory Services, the leading compliance consulting firm, so I had an affinity for these issues and was quite curious as to what he did.

What he did was staggering: he forgot to offer a form to one of his two hundred clients and forgot just once. Ironically, or not, he forgot to make the annual offer of his form ADV to one of his clients that past year. And for that, he must tell everyone he knows and will know he "violated a state law" and do it for ten years? This in my mind was one of the biggest examples of horribly poor regulator misconduct. This poor guy forgot just once to hand out a form to just one of his clients. And for that he's branded for a decade as a law-breaker? Simply horrible. Now if an advisor "forgets" to notify all his clients for one, two, three years... then we have a very sloppy person, and perhaps where "there is smoke, there is fire." That kind of poor management would justify a decade long admission of being a rule violator. There were a few things I took away from this experience:

1. The state either had an overly aggressive or very inexperienced regulator visit this advisor—neither are acceptable.

2. While this regulator was busy punishing this advisor needlessly, he or she was not spending time trying to find a truly bad advisor.

3. The advisor had to spend time dealing with this regulator, and one would assume spending less time taking care of clients.

4. For the period of ten years, how many of this advisor's clients may leave him? How many prospects who need help will not hire him be-

cause of that scary language? How is this actually helping the constituents of Pennsylvania? It's not; it's only hurting them.

5. Finally, its pays to read the actual disclosures if there are any for an advisor you are contemplating. What you read could very well be a significant factor in your hiring decision.

THEY THOUGHT WE WERE THE FEDS

From the summer of 1995 to the fall of 2001, I was the Director of Sales at National Regulatory Services, Inc. (NRS) in Lakeville, Connecticut. The firm provided services and software to help RIAs, broker-dealers, insurance firms, and mutual funds comply with all the various rules and regulations. It was the largest firm of its kind, and one of the oldest. When I joined there were roughly a dozen or so other firms around the country doing the same work. When Thomson Publishing, the international conglomerate, acquired them in 1999, there were many dozens more and today there are many hundreds of such firms. In short, complying with the securities rules has become very high in priority for financial advisors of all kinds. It is important to know that regulators almost never remove regulations; they usually only add new regulations year after year.

During my time at NRS, I learned an enormous amount. It was a time of significant change in regulatory compliance. I worked with hundreds of client firms, from the giants to literal startups. In my six years, I was aware of only three firms that looked "fishy" and we felt they were trying to hire us for some disingenuous reason. The rest had a genuine interest in working to comply with the regulations required of them.

One amazing lesson was a sales trip that illustrated for me the unhealthy dynamic between the regulators and those they regulate. I was in Milwaukee, Wisconsin, seeing clients and prospects and had a new sales executive with me that I was training. Our last meeting had just ended, it was 4:00 p.m. and we noticed in the next building a broker-dealer on the ground floor whose name I recognized. They were not a client, and we had no real relationship with them, so I decided we'd make a good old-fashioned face to face "cold call," as it's called.

The two of us were tired, wearing typical blue suits and carrying briefcases. In retrospect, we were dressed plainly. We walked in and I went to the receptionist and said without a smile, "Hi, can we please see your chief compliance officer?"

The blood ran out of her face, she got up, muttered something and went into a back office. Moments later two men came out walking quickly, straightening their ties and one introduced himself as the chief compliance officer and told me his name. Then it dawned on me: They must think we are government agents from the SEC! For a nanosecond, I thought, wow, this is the best sales approach in this business to get someone's attention. You scare them to death, then bring them back to life with the truth. Then I thought better.

"I am so sorry," I said, "We are not regulators; we are sales executives from NRS and just wanted to introduce ourselves." Like in a movie and on cue, their collective and very audible sigh of relief was amazing. And ridiculously funny. "Can we get you guys coffee, anything, anything at all?" they asked us. We all got a huge laugh out of it, as they genuinely were scared and so relieved we were not the Feds.

Over the years, I heard from so many clients—and from other chief compliance officers at brokerage firms—that most often the regulators immediately adopted an antagonistic attitude, did not know much about the industry, and worse, they drove you crazy with requests for information and documents that really were a waste of time and money. This was the collective experience of most of the regulated.

The big takeaway for me is that the ripple effect of having such an unhealthy relationship between the regulated and the regulators affects the consumer albeit in an indirect way. There is vital time, energy, and money that is pulled away from the consumer and diverted to regulatory compliance that is off point. If the rules are smart and the enforcers of the rules are industry experts at the top of their game, then not only will the very small number of bad actors get caught faster, the entire industry will expend less on needless rules, and use that time to focus on the client.

DEPARTMENT OF LABOR VERSUS SECURITIES AND EXCHANGE COMMISSION

Much has been written about the Department of Labor's rule to make all financial advice and sales of investment products in retirement accounts, including IRAs, fall under the fiduciary standard, as opposed to the less stringent suitability standard. In 2015, The White House Counsel of Economic Advisers estimated that seventeen billion dollars is lost annually due to biased advice. The department of labor wrote a one-thousand-plus page legislation that outlined their proposed rules. In recent months, courts have opined that the Department of Labor overreached their authority. Many economists and university professors have challenged the substance and numbers quoted in the legislation, and as expected, the financial industry is quite divided about the proposed law, the implementation of which has been delayed pending more review.

It is admirable that the Department of Labor wants to save investors money; however, its ability to govern all advisors is not clear, and the SEC is currently reviewing standards of advice. Because of this confusion and lack of coordination between regulators, investors and the industry are confused. Firms have changed procedures based on the rule, but then others have not because of the delay of implementation. This confusion has begun to have real-world impact on investors. I have a sister whose retirement account was altered without any advance notice by a large firm quoting "implementation of the Department of Labor rules." To be fair, the firm did a poor job of customer service, but not all firms are reacting the same…which is a result of regulators not coordinating.

In another example: according to the DOL rules, no one can invest in an IPO (Initial Public Offering) anymore in your own IRA. Many executives in the industry are in an uproar over this one, and as an investor, I find it highly offensive that I am not allowed to buy something if I choose to. To reiterate, any regulator who wants to protect investors and save them money are to be applauded; however, the rules need to be practical and uniform to prevent the kind of confusion and ill will we are currently experiencing.

JANUARY 2018: MOST ADVISORS ARE NOT ALLOWED TO TEXT CLIENTS

It has been widely reported that the very first text message was sent on December 3, 1992, by Neil Papworth in the United Kingdom. Today, 81 percent of Americans text regularly, according to the Pew Research Center, which number over six billion texts per day according to www.textrequest.com.

Using text messaging is not news; in fact, it might be a dying technology with services like Snapchat and other messaging products that are being developed. Yet, in the financial services sectors, text messaging is still making news. In a highly touted announcement on January 11, 2018, industry trade journal *On Wall Street* broke the news that Merrill Lynch would allow its advisors to text clients:

"Texting is just our latest investment in building our state-of-the-art digital capabilities so that we can serve our clients when, where and how they want," the announcement stated.

For most industries and companies there is no prohibition on texting a client; in fact, more communication with clients is generally encouraged to increase customer service. In the financial services world, permission to text was ground breaking news! The industry is in the stone ages compared to other industries, and financial services is a serious business. More than most people, I understand this. I am also aware that nearly fifty years ago we put a man on the moon and brought him back alive using technology that is primitive by today's standards. Allowing advisors to text safely should be easy, and should have been done many, many years ago.

Another broker-dealer followed suit within a week, and industry pundits predicted other firms will soon allow texting. Texting is not the only modern technology that was late in implementation by the financial advice world. Nearly every type of social media and electronic communication is regulated by government organizations in an effort to protect investors from false advertising, overpromising, and other abuses. Social media like LinkedIn and Facebook have only been allowed for roughly five years, as one example. When Twitter was first allowed, only pre-written tweets were allowed by the major firms. Kind of defeated the entire reason for Twitter!

The list of typical communication, social media, and marketing techniques that are not allowed by this industry is long. It has long been a point of major frustration by financial advisors of all types. The regulators are genuinely concerned with protecting investors, however, they largely miss the broader point of the ill effects of hampering communication between advisor and the investor. They certainly make no effort in helping the industry both comply and communicate.

The regulators don't want the industry to create ads that could be perceived as promising future results, overpromise what a particular investment might do, or even allow happy clients appear in ads. The premise of protection is admirable. The execution of locking down the industry to a series of open fields, green trees, and a "better tomorrow" in their ads communicates absolutely nothing.

By hampering communication, the regulators are actually preventing investors from getting educated. You will almost never see an ad from an advisory firm or brokerage firm that shows a successful client. I believe this is a huge mistake and makes American consumers ignorant beyond measure. The SEC and FINRA are happy to share on their websites about the latest scammer they sued, or taking Mark Cuban to court (and losing), but a happy, positive experience and outcome you do not see. What they do not seem to understand is basic human emotion: when all you see is negative, what is a person to perceive?

Now, if most advisors were crooks, then their approach would make sense. But that is not the case and never was. Only a very small percentage of all advisors run afoul of the rules and law. Why, then, are they treated as if it is the opposite? The answer is simple: very old laws enforced by regulators that, for the most part, have never actually worked in this industry. Both need to change.

The vast majority of investor experiences are positive ones. Sharing the positive along with the negative will help better educate the investor.

CHAPTER 11

THE MEDIA LOVES TO BASH

The media are partially responsible for the misconceptions and the negative images of financial advisors. Can you recall the last time you read a positive story about advisors? I'm sure there are some, but it would take digging to find them. I bet you can recall reading a negative article about advisors. Now, juxtapose that with the fact that only a small percentage of financial advisors were penalized by regulators.

MY FIRSTHAND EPIPHANY

Several years ago, as CEO of a startup, I was promoting a very new cutting edge application that involved investors and advisors. We had a public relations firm that took me to see many of the New York financial media. We met with nearly every household-named publication, website, and a number of cable and TV stations. We had a standard opening message about the marketplace of advisors and shared that advisors in general are misunderstood. I shared that at that time only 7 percent of all financial and insurance advisors as a combined number had any negative history. At first, in nearly all the meetings, I heard the exact same refrain "Interesting...now tell me about a bad advisor!" I literally had to prepare a statement for future meetings that went something like this: "Given only 7 percent of advisors have some negative history, for the hour we have together, I'll allocate 7 percent of our time to the negative stories, and 93 percent of our time to the positive stories, does that sound fair?" This consistent interest in the negative forced me to the conclusion that if the only stories investors see in the media are negative, in the absence of virtually no positive stories, then what is the consumer to believe? After this experience I came to the conclusion that the media is one of the drivers of a negative narrative, despite the facts telling us otherwise.

To be fair, it is vitally important for the media to report news, which does educate, especially when crimes are being committed. However, there are thousands of positive stories about advisors which are newsworthy. There needs to be balance that reflects the statistics of reality.

Why the downer approach? Positive headlines supposedly don't draw readers in droves. But negative ones are gobbled up because of our purported insatiable appetite for stories about crooks and frauds. What better proof than the Hollywood blockbusters and TV crime series that draw big audiences? Are our values askew, or are we easily bored? I'll let my readers answer that question rather than take the position of moral or ethical arbiter.

JOURNALISTS

In the February 2, 2018, "Your Money" column in the *New York Times*, Ron Lieber wrote in the article "Yes, You Can Find a Financial Planner Even if You're Not Rich" that:

"But an ugly fact of the financial advice industry has generally been this: There are precious few practitioners who will work with people that are not wealthy, or at least not without pushing questionable, commission-laden investments and insurance policies."

Ron's statement is patently incorrect. To begin with, there are, and have been for decades, thousands of financial planners all around the country who work with the unwealthy and charge low fees. Shockingly, one company president Ron was interviewing for his article worked for a firm that had been offering reasonably priced financial plans since 2002, a full sixteen years. Moreover, starting in 1991—while working at Waterhouse Securities, (now TD Ameritrade)—I met many such planners face to face at meetings of the National Association of Personal Financial Advisors (NAPFA), a trade association of fee-only advisors, as well as other trade associations such as the predecessor associations of the Financial Planning Association. A number of these advisors charge a modest fee for hourly planning. Secondly, as the co-founder and CEO of the two largest advisor-data companies, Discovery Data and Meridian-IQ, I directly acquired data on all the nations Registered Investment Advisers from the Securities and Exchange Commission (SEC) and State Regulators. The data shows there are thousands that offer planning work for an hourly fee.

Secondly, his statement "or at least not without pushing questionable, commission-laden investments and insurance policies" is wildly ignorant and misleads the reader. There are tens of thousands of advisors and millions of clients who are having their needs optimally served with a quality investment that just so happens to carry a commission. A plan that is paid for via commission instead of a fee is not by itself indicative of a lesser service. There are millions of investors who have simple needs and some of history's best net performing funds can carry a commission; in fact, they can be less expensive than paying a fee. Post Department of Labor adoption data is starting to prove this. Finally, Ron omits the historic fact that the insurance world gave birth to modern financial planning, and advising on insurance is a mandatory component of today's financial planning profession.

Ron goes on to praise two terrific organizations in the article, which I also write about very positively in this book. But at the same time, he insinuates in wholesale fashion to the reader that anyone other than members of these two organizations should be avoided. This article is one of hundreds like it published in just the past few years that does not truly educate the reader, and therefore, creates misinformation in the minds of consumers. For purposes of full disclosure, for decades I have always looked forward to reading the weekend edition of the *New York Times*. Like many in my age bracket, I regret seeing such a fine publication shrink in size year after year, so I have no issue with the *Times* itself.

Direct from a Journalist

The following is taken directly from Andy Gluck's "Advisors4Advisors" blog published on March 6, 2013. Andy is a well-known former consumer and industry journalist, entrepreneur, and marketing expert:

"There is a longstanding tradition in personal finance journalism to bash financial advisors. I did it when I was at *The New York Daily News* in the 1980s and *Worth* in the 1990s. Back then, the world was simple. You could bash the vast majority of advisors, but you could also refer people to fee-only advisors and hold them out as being a solution to the financial advice problem faced by consumers.

"The world has since become much more complicated. Fee-only is no longer a guarantee of ethical, knowledgeable, and caring financial advice. Yes, the vast majority of fee-only advisors are the good guys, but enough of the bad guys have infiltrated the fee-only model to ruin it for the good guys. As a result, a growing trend toward bashing the entire profession has been emerging. (And the press has no ability or inclination to discern that some advisors who take commissions are also honest and knowledgeable.)

"Advisors should speak out against this naïve coverage. Keep in mind that the consumer press is here to sell papers and magazines and ads online. It is in their interest to empower consumers to invest on their own. Their goal is to tell clients how to do what you do. Their goal is to make it sound simple and tell people they can read their content and not pay an advisor. Advisors should respond to the growing trend toward bashing the entire profession. In fact, doing so presents an opportunity. "By responding to personal finance reporters who smear advisors, by commenting on blogs and posting your own videos and articles that tell your story and demonstrate your commitment to provide advice ethically, you will increase your search engine visibility. By publicly responding with information about investment fiduciaries, you will help educate the press and investors. Plus, it will boost your credibility with people who know if you stand up for what you believe."

Newspapers

Even the *Wall Street Journal's* coverage of financial advisors has its issues. A few years ago, the newspaper had a front-page business section story. It was unusual because they had a follow-up story the very next day, again front page of the business section, below the fold. It was an investigative piece that researched the disciplinary history of brokers by obtaining FINRA (the broker regulator) data on many, but not all, brokers. The basic premise of the article was that there were brokers who had significant negative regulatory history, such as dozens of fines, arbitrations, and complaints, yet they were still in the industry, and worse yet, moved from firm to firm. These firms had many such bad advisors. I feel very comfortable calling these advisors bad because if you have dozens of fines paid over a ten-year career, there is no other way to be described.

What was very misleading about these two articles is that they started the pieces with incredibly troubling statistics about these advisors, they ended the pieces with the same level of scary language and statistics, but only in the middle of these very long articles was the classic "to be fair" statement, which shows the other side of the equation. And in a sentence or two, the authors shared that of all the broker data found, a very small number had any negative history—7 percent of the brokers. Which, as I have shared earlier in this book, is essentially the same rate as doctors and attorneys. What people remember from any article is the first couple of paragraphs and the last couple paragraphs, and I found it to be troubling that the impression of the entire industry was filled with bad actors.

To be clear, I am a proponent of investigative journalism, and ferreting out and removing bad actors in any industry. However, it should be done in a balanced way that truly educates the reader as to the entirety of the industry and not leave the reader with a statistically unbalanced view of the market.

Movies and TV

I hate to admit it, but there are many great movies about Wall Street scandals and bad advisors. Some of the more popular movies in no particular order are: *Wall Street* and its years-later sequel *Wall Street: Money Never Sleeps, Boiler Room, The Wolf of Wall Street, Margin Call, The Big Short, Money Monster, Equity, Too Big to Fail, Rogue Trader, Other People's Money, Working Girl,* and *Arbitrage*. These, of course, are just the films whose entire plot revolves around financial services. There are many more movies where a supporting actor works in financial services and is an unlikeable character.

In all these movies, the basic theme is someone in the course of their professional work is violating some law or regulation to get ahead financially. While the drama and suspense is undeniably entertaining, it is also undeniable that the tone of the movie is quite negative. Over the course of time, a movie fan can only be left with the impression that financial advisors and Wall Street is not an industry that does positive work. Even if you do not think one has a negative impression of the industry, it is inarguable that none of these movies illustrate anything positive about being a financial advisor or working on Wall Street.

Television and cable TV are the least of the offenders in the media of an unbalanced narrative about financial advisors. There is the occasional exposé about fraud involving financial advisors, such as CNBC's "American Greed," but they cover all fashion of criminals, and sometimes, a financial advisor.

Advertising by Full Service Firms

This category is not caused per se by the media itself, but rather, basic economics. Every day we are exposed to advertising and content that is generated by those firms that use their marketing dollars for national advertising. It is the largest of firms like Merrill Lynch, Morgan Stanley, Wells Fargo, UBS, and to a lesser extent firms, like Ameriprise, Edward Jones, and Raymond James. There is nothing wrong with these ads; in fact, they are generally very good ads.

The issue is that what we get, for the most part, is the impression that you need to have significant wealth to use some of these firms. More to the point is what we do not see in the media every day, which is the literal hundreds of thousands—by most estimates it is three hundred thousand or so financial advisors—who work at firms that do not have advertising budgets. These are often firms that cater to smaller investors. The mere absence of smaller advisors in the daily media mix over the course of time develops a lack of understanding that these firms exist. This is not a negative in the absolute, but it becomes a negative when one considers the fact that smaller investors and consumers can get the help they need, yet don't, out of sheer lack of knowing there are advisors available to them.

Advertising by Discount Brokers

Again, this category of misperception is not caused by the media itself; rather, we consume this content in the media, which is worth noting. Super Bowl ads, cable TV, and network advertising by discount brokers is nothing new. But sometimes ads—especially ones that are very eye-catching, provocative, and viral—can create conflicting messages that damage the investor-advisor interaction. The E-Trade "Don't Get Mad" ad shows people getting jealous at very wealthy co-workers, former school mates, and the like. The solution of course is "Don't Get Mad" and then open an account at E-Trade and become wealthy like others by trading your own account. I think this particular ad series is very troubling because any decent advisor will tell you that trading, day trading, or even buy and hold investing, will not get you rich anytime soon.

Most advisors will also tell you that it is very difficult to beat the market over the long haul. The vast majority of mutual funds do not beat the indexes, so an individual investor trading for their own account has indeed a tough hill to climb if they think investing will get them wealthy quickly. On this point too, the ad insinuates the individual investor can beat the markets and the professionals, which is obviously a very dangerous message.

While the ad does not blatantly say this, the visual message is that you can catch up to that high school jerk, who is now a billionaire with a yacht. This ad series, while artistically terrific and funny, are doing damage by relaying an unrealistic message. Unrealistic messages are by definition the antithesis of what most financial advisors provide.

E-Trade has another ad, the "This is Getting Old," campaign which illustrates that many Americans still no not have enough money saved for retirement. The visuals are people in the eighties still working hard, and the message is, if you don't save now you will never retire. This ad campaign is very good and positively reinforces the benefits of saving by giving the viewer a picture into the future if you do not save. It is the exact same message that most advisors give their clients, so in this case, it is a positively reinforcing message.

Another point on these ads that is missed by many is that they focus on investing, which is what discount brokers do; they allow you to buy and sell stock, bonds, options, ETFs, open-ended funds, and a whole plethora of investments. However, investing may not be the most important thing for many investors. For many viewers, insurance, cash flow, or debt reduction, might be the most important financial action to take, yet there are no ads for these services generally speaking. The media shows almost all investing ads, but the other aspects of your financial health (i.e. a financial plan), are not advertised. Viewers of these ads are only seeing one aspect of their financial health, which is not healthy over the course of time. The viewer may be lulled into thinking the only area to focus on is investing. To reiterate, the advertiser is doing their job; it's up to the consumer to realize they are only seeing a part of reality.

CHAPTER 12

SEARCHING FOR YOUR FINANCIAL ADVISOR

There is bad news and good news when you're searching for a financial advisor. The bad news is that there is, remarkably, no one singular listing of all the nation's financial advisors that is suitable for consumer use. I know quite a lot about compiling lists of all the nation's advisors, as I have built and was the founding CEO of the two largest such firms. The difference was that I built these directories for institutions to use, not consumers.

The baseline data for an institutional use of such a directory comes from a huge volume of regulatory data. This raw data, once compiled and organized, is used by mutual fund companies, technology firms, and recruiters who are looking to sell things to these advisors. The data they care about resides in this raw regulatory data. However, the information a consumer cares about is not in this data. Therefore, these databases that actually include every advisor are nearly useless to consumers. I know this first hand as I tried to market this data to consumers and it failed. My competitors in the institutional market also tried to market it to consumers, and again, no takers. There are a number of commercial directories that are attempting to market to consumers today and fall far short of being useful. They either have regulatory data exclusively, which really tells the consumer nothing of differential value, or they are opt-in directories that have a very small population of advisors, and to make matters worse, the data is not fact-checked. When I have looked at these existing data sources, they are not effective. Perhaps one day someone will come up with a truly useful directory for consumers.

The good news comes in two parts. One, there are several trade associations that list their members freely for consumers to search. Many of the larger firms also have a search function on their websites. Two, most of today's advisors want to be found via Google searches. At the end of this chapter, I share these sites, combined with Google searches, and explain how to understand and use this two-part tactic to create a list of advisors who may meet your needs. One caveat about the listings and directories is that none of them are perfectly complete. In some cases, the advisor simply does not care to be a part of a directory listing, they do not belong to a trade group, or they don't pay to be a member of a for-profit network. However, by using both these directories and Google, you will have access to more than enough advisors to create a list and begin the narrowing process to find someone right for you.

When you combine this with chapter 13, on how to how to spot and avoid a bad advisor, and chapter 14, on how to interview advisors, you will be fully prepared to find your perfect financial advisor. This process does require a little time on your part, but the time taken is more than worth the effort.

ASKING YOUR FRIENDS AND FAMILY FOR AN ADVISOR REFERRAL

Nearly all consumers and investors have found their advisors through personal referral in one way or another. You ask your parents, your boss, and your friends who they use. You know or meet someone in a familiar setting such at Rotary meeting, Chamber of Commerce meeting, or house of worship. Your CPA or your attorney has worked with someone for years and has high regard for the advisor and refers to them. There can be a problem with this method of finding an advisor in that acquaintances who you personally trust usually do not fully understand the advisor they are referring you to. They often say, "I have known him for years; he is a terrific guy. I am very happy." Or "I have been sending my clients to her for years. We really work well together."

Rarely will you hear in great specificity what *exactly* this advisor does for a living, his or her specialty, their niche, if they have troubling negative regulatory history, their belief systems in terms of investment philosophy, designations, or work history, all which makes them unique. It's the very reason I am writing this book: people simply do not understand advisors. Thus, when receiving a referral from others, be open to the possibility that your friend may not be fully aware of the advisor they are referring you to. Make sure you follow the steps in the chapters on spotting a bad advisor and interviewing advisors when evaluating personal referrals.

Before I share the specific process to create your advisor short list, I want to share some additional investor stories, as I find that real life stories are very educational and can help you think more broadly and creatively about who to look for.

Most of the investor stories are from complete strangers, people that were sent to me by others. I had no idea what they were going to tell me, and I simply asked them to tell me their financial story, whether it involved an advisor or not. Remember that there are many millions of investors and consumers that have used the hundreds of thousands of financial advisors to help solve their particular issue.

DIVORCING WOMEN

Margaret (not her real name) is in her late thirties and went through a personal and financial rollercoaster because of a bad first marriage. Her story, while upsetting, is not unheard of. Her former husband essentially tried to blackmail her into staying in a bad marriage by making subtle threats that her credit would get ruined should they divorce. They jointly owned a house and had a large line of credit based on the equity in the home. As the relationship deteriorated, her husband depleted the entire line of credit for his personal use, and to make matters worse, he got laid off and did not make payments on the loan.

During and after the divorce, he continued to stick her with the bills. The home value plummeted as most did during the 2008 housing crash, so refinancing was not possible, and eventually, Margaret was forced to allow the home to be foreclosed on. Through friends and her own tough experience, Margaret shared with me several lessons that others can benefit from. First, she should have left the marriage earlier. Second, upon noticing the signs her husband was going to use financial coercion, she should have squirreled away money in her own account earlier and in greater amounts. Finally, she is thankful to have always kept a credit card in her name only.

During our conversation, I shared with Margret that there are hundreds of mostly-female advisors who cater to women going through divorce. These advisors not only know the best money practices for divorcing women, but also become an emotional support system. They have seen and helped hundreds of others go through this traumatic period. Margret wished she was aware of these types of advisors when she was going through her terrible time. Happily, Margaret is now remarried to a terrific guy who is financially responsible. She shared that while it sounded trite, the many people who told her it would be better in the end, were right.

PAYING FOR COLLEGE

Amrinder Babbra is the co-founder of the nonprofit, nonpartisan International Behavioral Research Institute based in Chicago, Illinois. He received his master's degree in behavior analysis and therapy, and is currently pursuing a PhD in the same course of study at the Rehabilitation Institute at Southern Illinois University. In 1990, he was born in a small village near Hoshiarpur, India. Amrinder's family came to the U.S when he was two. His mother was the primary breadwinner, as his father had a chronic condition that prevented him from working. Despite her difficulty with English, Amrinder's mother quickly exhibited her intellect in many ways, one of which was finances. In this regard, she was an excellent role model for Amrinder and his sister. When he was twelve, she taught them about managing a checkbook, internet banking, and credit cards. She purchased life insurance for her son and daughter when they were fifteen and sixteen, a highly unusual but very savvy move. She purchased a home and navigated the financial crisis of 2008 successfully and—unlike many others—came out unscathed presumably because, among other things, she understood the potential consequences of her mortgage agreement.

One of the drivers for Amrinder to learn serious financial responsibility was the unusual and, one would assume, emotionally stressful situation of his father being unable to work. He had to learn finances out of necessity; it was not by choice. By the time he got to college, he was much more adept at managing his personal finances than most of his peers. He knew the dangers of credit card debt and knew how to make the most of better offers and balance transfer tactics. In school, his interest in finance was fueled by interactions with his professors, and also by his interest in the application of behavior analysis to personal finance.

Despite all the excellent financial training he received from his mother and from his own personal interest, he had a financial blind spot when it came to college tuition. He was aware of advisors that catered to the need of college funding. However, due to a combination of mistrust and the lack of availability at the time, he did not hire one. He believes the calculus of college costs versus anticipated earnings was not considered, partly due to cultural pressure and stigmas in the Indian culture. Going to a four-year university is something that was assumed and expected in his community.

In hindsight, he still questions the debt and school decisions that stem from these pervasive social stigmas. Due to these experiences, he now believes others should weigh more seriously the alternatives of free local schools, or an associate degree to start with the possibility transferring to a four-year school. Thankfully,

Amrinder has been able to refinance his school debt through the Common Bond organization for a lower monthly expense. In retrospect, had he been able to better anticipate these setbacks, he would have stepped out of his comfort zone and sought out a financial advisor that catered to college funding to give a different perspective and weigh the options.

Amrinder has a deep, passionate interest in human behavior, because at the crux of poor financial decisions is individual behavior, which is why he is sharing his personal experience. During our conversation, he was surprised to learn that there were non-profit organizations that gave financial advice for free to those in need. This was fascinating due to his incredibly thorough research into personal finance. He shared his personal story in the hopes of helping others cope with, weigh the costs and benefits of, and ultimately, make an educated and informed decision on education. Amrinder hopes that by sharing his personal experience he can help an entirely different set of people.

CONSOLIDATION OF RETIREMENT ACCOUNTS

Marie has worked for over twenty years since graduating from college. She contributed to her past employers' 401(k) accounts consistently but never had an advisor during her working career. In her forties, she married and had children and started to think more seriously about retirement. She had many IRAs and 401ks from multiple employers and investment firms, but had no idea where to start.

She has a friend who is knowledgeable about investments and financial advice and he recommended she get an hourly or flat-fee financial planner to look at her current investments and make sense of them. He provided her with a short list of hourly financial planners to contact. She contacted them and chose the one that she felt most comfortable with based on how their initial phone conversation went. The planner charges by the hour and is fee-only, meaning she receives no compensation from any fund company. The planner wanted to meet in person and sent a list of things Marie would need to bring to the meeting.

At the meeting, the planner reviewed all of Marie's statements and accounts and asked about her desires for the future. There were two main messages the planner gave Marie. First, she needed to save much more money each year to ensure a comfortable retirement. Second, she needed to consolidate all the disparate accounts into two retirement accounts, a Roth IRA and a Traditional IRA, and move all the disparate funds into one lower cost target date fund. The new fund is sponsored by a very well-known large fund company that has many low cost, well performing funds. However, Marie was not given a clear indication from the planner on the exact annual cost savings the new fund would provide, versus the former funds she has.

The planner gave instructions on exactly how to open the two new accounts and transfer the funds from the current mutual funds into the new fund. The instructions were sent via email and, in retrospect, were not well organized and not completely clear. It took Marie a number of hours and several weeks to get all the monies transferred and turned out to be a fairly frustrating process, as each fund company had slightly different procedures for transferring money out of their companies. For some firms, the funds would be sent directly to the new mutual fund company. For others, they would only send the check to Marie, who in turn had to send that check to the new fund company.

After a few weeks, the entire process was completed. Marie spent three hundred dollars for two hours of the planner's time and now has just two accounts to focus on, with the same fund company. She is relieved that she has consolidated her accounts and now her focus is to work on saving more.

SEMI SELF-DIRECTED

Ron (real first name, his last name he preferred to not share) wrote to me to share his experiences with financial advisors. The following is almost verbatim, aside from some non-material editing:

"I have a financial advisor and I trust him. I've had other advisors through the years. Most were good, but nothing more. I had one that was excellent and then there's my current guy who is beyond excellent. Through the years, I've learned quite a bit about investing and I often steer my portfolio according to my market anticipations. However, when I was young, I was very mistrustful of others. It was only with experience and age that I overcame my prejudice against financial advisors. Part of my turnaround might be due to my own fortunes—once you pass a certain threshold of wealth there's no avoiding some form of financial advice.

"My first exposure to a financial advisor was back in the late '70s. My parents were investing in the money market and getting really good returns. I only remember the advisor as an elderly man and my father insisting that his investment money should be 'safe.' Once the CD boom ended the money got parked into a conservative tax-free fund that never generated much return. The advisor passed away and my parents never moved the money from the fund. But they complained about the lack of return and how you couldn't trust these financial guys. (Looking back at it now, I realize they got exactly what they asked for: something very safe.)

"But that was my parents' experience, not mine. I was in my thirties and was my own advisor. I had a small nest egg but, due to my parents' experience, I distrusted financial advisors. I lived and worked in New York City at the time. I attempted to learn about investing, but had little time for it. I bit the bullet and contacted an advisor. He was young and aggressive enough to make me doubt his advice. I suppose I feared he would steal my money.

"I knew I wanted to buy stock in a company large enough not to go bust and small enough to get a short-term profit. I did some reading about a sugar refiner called "Sucrest" (now known as Ingredient Technology Corporation). They had signed a long-term contract with some nation in the Caribbean and were in the process of negotiating long-term contracts with a cane supplier in the Philippines. Some Sucrest historical info mentioned bad profits due to a Caribbean hurricane unexpectedly increasing the price of raw cane. I reasoned that the chances of a Caribbean hurricane and a Philippine typhoon occurring in the same year were remote and I liked the idea of the company paying a steady price for raw cane. So, I decided to go all-in on Sucrest and watched it rise from ten to twenty over a year. It then started a slow decline, dipping as low as twelve but then rebounding. I sold at 14 making a 40 percent profit in two years, which was fine with me. That's how I managed to buy my first house at age thirty.

"In 1990 I was contacted by a financial advisor from Eaton Vance. He was pushing Oracle as an investment and used some shady math to prove his point. (I have a background in engineering so I can spot bad math when I see it.) I said no thank you. Little did I know that this young man, despite the bad math, had actually given me excellent advice. Oracle stock was just beginning a steady rise that lasted a decade. But, not knowing the future, I decided to invest in CDs. (A poor investment choice at the time.)

"I had no financial advisor until after I retired. By then my parents had died and I sold their house. I needed to do something with the money. In 2004 a local financial advisor from Edward Jones knocked on my door. My wife and I liked him, so we decided to invest some money with him. The returns were acceptable so we invested some more. Eventually we put almost all of our money in. The first advisor got a promotion and moved to NYC. We were assigned a new advisor and my wife and I were worried. The new guy wanted to restructure our investments. He wanted us more global and less USA-based.

"Meanwhile I had been reading the monthly Edward Jones magazine and I had started watching Jim Cramer on TV. I had my own Scottrade account and was doing slightly better than the Edward Jones account. I fancied that I now 'understood' the market. (Deluded fool!) I found myself agreeing with the new advisor's investment ideas. He recommended diversifying my portfolio, becoming

135

more international. In fact I overloaded my account with international companies and my advisor thought this as wise. This strategy paid off and the returns became stunning. He found some really good bonds for me too. After several years he rebalanced me from mostly international to more U.S.-based and, once again, the returns were great. Lately he's taken a fair amount of money out of the stock market and put it into CDs and bonds.

"I'm probably not a typical investor. My relationship with my advisor is this: I tend to be too aggressive and he tempers my choices. We study the account every year and, if the investments get too skewed in any particular direction, we re-balance. If the market gets very volatile my advisor always calls. I'm very happy with him. As I get older I'm less inclined to push my account towards my opinions and more receptive to my advisor's advice."

START YOUR SEARCH

Before you search for your first financial advisor, or a new financial advisor, you must ask yourself why you believe you need a financial advisor in the first place. If you have no idea, but feel like getting help is smart, your advisor search is actually the easiest, so read on.

For everyone else, you should write down what your issue is and be as specific as possible. It could be saving for retirement, help managing a portfolio of stocks, or paying for your children's college. Whatever your need is, simply write it down so it is documented. Save it, as you'll need to reflect on it later.

As you will see, I often suggest adding your city and state to the search criteria. The reason for this is all else being equal, it is preferable to have someone physically close to you. There are many dimensions to this concept of locality, but to begin with, your perfect financial advisor may very well be halfway across the world from you and all will be perfectly fine.

Still, having an advisor close to you is preferable for a number of reasons. First, being able to meet your advisor, look in their eyes, see how they dress, and see their office, is valuable information if you know how to process it. In the chapter on interviewing advisors, I go into all this. Also, seeing your advisor periodically through the year can be very informative. Seeing them and their conduct in the community, their family, and other aspects of their life is helpful. Be aware, however, that the slickest con men have used community to their advantage to unsuspecting victims. This I also show in the chapter on how to spot a bad advisor.

On the flip side, your advisor seeing you regularly can help the advisor deliver great financial advice over the course of time. A great advisor will politely nudge you to stop procrastinating on what action you may have not implemented. Your advisor bumping into you at the pool store seeing you purchase chlorine can be a big deal if your advisor was unaware that you just installed a new built-in pool and you never changed your homeowner's or personal liability policy, not to mention to higher taxes in the coming year that may impact your plan.

When I write, "all else being equal," it's really a generalization...because nothing is ever equal in life or in finding an advisor. But the tiebreaker in picking your perfect advisor could be locality, so it's a factor.

If you are comfortable with it, I would use an Excel spreadsheet to create your list. If not, a lined paper pad will suffice. Give yourself room under each entry to make notes.

I HAVE NO IDEA HOW TO IMPROVE MY FINANCIAL LIFE

If you do not know how to begin to improve your financial life, then you should get a financial plan. This is the best thing you can do for yourself, as you will assuredly learn something that you never even knew to ask yourself. To get a financial plan, you need a financial planner. There are a number of sources to get a list of financial planners. There is overlap, as most planners are CFPs, but the other organizations members focus on a certain niche of client or business practice.

CFP Board: This is the certification board of the CFP designation with over seventy thousand planners holding the designation. http://www.letsmakeaplan.org

NAPFA: All NAPFA members have the CFP designation, however NAPFA members are fee-only, meaning they do not believe in receiving any form of commission as part of their compensation. https://www.napfa.org/find-an-advisor

Garrett Planning Network: Garrett members are fee-only and serve middle market clients with hourly planning. https://www.garrettplanningnetwork.com

XY Planning Network: XY members cater to younger clients, are fee-only, and are CFPs. https://www.xyplanningnetwork.com/consumer/find-advisor/

I HAVE AN INVESTMENT PORTFOLIO TO MANAGE, BUT NO OTHER NEEDS

There is no consumer-focused inclusive directory to search for advisors that focus only on managing investment portfolios. Many, but not all, financial planners also manage portfolios. Investment management is a subset of financial planning, and the planning sites mentioned before can be a source.

Additional sources for advisors that manage money are these two organizations:

1. CFA Institute
   https://www.cfainstitute.org/community/membership/directory/

2. Investments & Wealth Institute
   https://investmentsandwealth.org/investors

In addition, there are many advisors that have been managing money for years and for one reason or another do not possess a designation. Google the terms "Asset Management" or "Investment Management" and your city and state, and look at the first three pages of results. It is important to get at least ten advisors in your city from all three sources, as some of them may focus on institutional clients, and not individuals. Moreover, some may have account minimums that do not match your investable asset level.

I NEED HELP WITH INVESTMENTS AND OTHER SPECIFIC ISSUES

When you need help with investing and other financial issues, the advisors that provide both services are called wealth managers. Please note this term is industry jargon, it is not a regulated term. There are some certifications that incorporate the term. Financial planners that also manage money are should be included in your search, as financial planners that also manage money are considered wealth managers. You should also google the term "Wealth Management" and your city and state, which will result in advisors that can be included on your initial list.

I HAVE A VERY SPECIFIC ISSUE OR GOAL

Financial planners from the listings mentioned before should be included; also, Googling that term plus your city and state will give you potential advisors to add to your list. For example, if you are a widow or know a widow who needs an advisor, then search the term "financial advisor widows (your city, your state)" and on the first three pages, advisors will come up that share those key words.

NOW YOU HAVE YOUR INITIAL LIST OF ADVISORS

By now, you likely have from ten to thirty or more advisors on a list. The task now is to eliminate advisors that we easily identify as not being right for you. To do this, you need to go to each advisor's website, and on the home page, read about the advisor's typical clients. Some of these advisors only work with institutions, so obviously delete them off your list. If your particular search is for help with your investment portfolio, try and find the advisor's minimum account size. Advisors do put this on their website, but some do not. Eliminate those that have a minimum that does not match your portfolio size.

ELIMINATE ADVISORS WITH UNACCEPTABLE NEGATIVE HISTORY

From here, you will want to check out the regulatory history of the advisors remaining on your list. The advisors are either regulated by FINRA, as they are broker-dealer reps, or they are regulated by the SEC/State as they are Registered Investment Advisers. If you are unsure who the regulator is, check both of these regulatory/government databases: https://brokercheck.finra.org/ https://www.adviserinfo.sec.gov/

What you are looking for is the section called "Disclosures," and that is where any negative information about the advisor is disclosed. Using this information to disqualify an advisor for you is very much a judgement call. When people ask my personal opinion, I like to disqualify anyone that has anything disclosed. However, this is a very conservative view. And to be fair, I have seen a lot of disclosures mandated by regulators that are nonsense, as I have written about in other sections of the book.

To reiterate, across all types of advisors including insurance advisors, about 7 percent of all advisors have something negative on record. Moreover, about half of the disclosures are non-events, and the other half, about 3 percent, are so bad that I believe those advisors should be barred from the industry.

When you see disclosures, use common sense. Fifteen disclosures in a twenty-year career is almost always an indicator of someone who uses bad judgement...or worse. One disclosure in a thirty-year career is probably fine, but it depends what the mistake was. You must read what the event is—the details are incredibly important. For example, I have seen advisors working at very large firms who have paid back monies to more than ten different clients over the years due to claims of mishandling of investments. I would never hire an advisor with this history. I saw a younger advisor who in his thirties, just one year prior to becoming an advisor, was arrested three times, once per year for three years running for misdemeanors such as DUI, evading arrest, and public drunkenness. I also would never hire this advisor. I have seen advisors at very small firms with multiple disclosures for violating a variety of regulatory rules. I also would not hire this advisor.

One final note about disclosures that is important to remember. It is possible to encounter an advisor that has no disclosures and he or she turns out to be a criminal. One of the more remarkable stories is a former president of a fee-only, fiduciary trade association who is currently serving a twelve-year sentence for fraud. At the time of his arrest, his regulatory records were completely clean. I go into greater detail about his particular case in another chapter, and the good news is that it is relatively easy to spot this fraud quickly, and either prevent yourself from being a victim, or catching it very early. To reiterate, only roughly 3 percent of advisors have such bad conduct, so the odds are very low you will ever meet one, but I will show you how to reduce your odds of ever encountering one.

Now you are ready to take your list of potential advisors and follow the practices in chapter 13 and 14.

CHAPTER 13

HOW TO SPOT AND AVOID BAD ADVISORS

What constitutes a "bad" advisor? For purposes of this chapter, I define "bad" as bad in the absolute, not a "bad for you, good for another consumer" definition. For example, we all have had dates that were horrible and really bad for us, but a wonderful match for someone else. No, in this chapter I am referring to an advisor that is pretty much bad for anyone. Thankfully that number is quite low, but you do not want to run the risk of being one of the unlucky that signs up with one.

As I have mentioned throughout this book, the vast majority of financial advisors are well-intentioned and honest professionals who seek to genuinely help their clients. Of all the advisors in the United States, 7 percent have some negative regulatory or legal event in their past, and roughly half of that 7 percent have very negative events…so much so that they likely should not be in the industry at all. Of course, statistics being what they are, it is very likely that there are some bad advisors who simply have not gotten caught yet, so likely the "bad actor" number could be higher than 7 percent. However, it is impossible to analyze the activity of close to two million financial and insurance advisors and their clients together, so we can only go by the public numbers we have to estimate the bad actor rates.

What this means is that 3percent of the advisors with very bad history should never be hired. This amounts to sixty thousand financial and insurance advisors in the U.S. How do you avoid one of these advisors? In this chapter, I outline the steps in order of priority of importance in order to protect yourself from hiring one of these bad actors. To be clear, this is a descending priority list, with the first step as most important, the second step as next important, and so on. It is vital you take each of these steps to minimize the odds of hiring a bad advisor.

Please note these steps cannot guarantee that you will avoid a bad advisor, but will give you the highest odds of avoiding one. There are two reasons for this caveat: one, there could be advisors that right now are conducting a new type of harmful service that simply no one has considered or found yet, such as some brand-new scheme or fraud that is the first of its kind. Second, there have been cases where a good advisor turned bad and you could hire an advisor that is perfectly legitimate and doing a good job for you, but then changes how he or she does things. Such a case was Mark Spangler, who I mention later in this chapter.

CRITICAL STEPS TO AVOID A BAD ADVISOR IN ORDER OF IMPORTANCE

1. Verify the person is actually licensed

Make sure your advisor is regulated by at least one of the regulators that oversees retail financial advisors. The SEC regularly states that one of the most common types of frauds are those committed by persons who are not in fact licensed financial advisors. If you are ever approached with an investment proposal by an unlicensed person, always have a licensed financial advisor review the investment. Here are the regulators to check to ensure the person you are speaking with is in fact licensed:

1. https://brokercheck.finra.org/

2. https://www.adviserinfo.sec.gov/IAPD/default.aspx

If you cannot find the advisor in one of these regulatory databases, do not hire the advisor. It is nearly impossible to legally give advice or sell a security without being registered by some regulatory authority. There are some very narrow exceptions, but for 99 percent of Americans, if they are not registered somewhere, do not use that person.

2. Check their regulatory background

Once you find your advisor, look at the section of their record called "disclosures." In short, this is where anything negative on the advisor is stored. The vast majority of advisors do not have any disclosures. That said, having a disclosure item does not mean the advisor is bad. However, the more disclosures an advisor has, the more scrutiny one should take in evaluating the advisor.

Pay special attention to disclosures where the advisor had to pay fines to a regulator or had to personally compensate a client due to a complaint. If there are more than a couple such instances, you should take extreme care in evaluating this advisor.

Finally, it is important to understand that there are plenty of occasions where an overzealous regulator will force a disclosure on an advisor, or a former employer can force a disclosure that are unfair and not an issue. This can make an otherwise great advisor look bad, so it is vital to understand the difference. Finally, there are occasions where an unreasonable client sued an advisor and it was far cheaper to simply settle the case and accept a disclosure than battle the client in court or arbitration. While I have always counseled an advisor to fight the client in these cases, the reality is sometimes the advisor simply cannot afford a legal battle that has an unknown cost and it ends up being the only disclosure over an entire career. These scenarios happened right after the market meltdown of 2008 and I saw first-hand wonderful advisors get unfairly blamed for a market correction

Here is a breakdown of categories of disclosures:

1. Client

A client can complain about an investment gone bad, theft, bad advice, or nearly literally any kind of grievance. When these escalate they can end up on the advisor's record and stay there either in perpetuity or for some lesser period of time. In order to get on the record, usually the advisor's employer or their regulator forces the disclosure. In the case of a Registered Investment Adviser, they are required to self-disclose, and if they do not, the penalties are quite severe.

2. Regulatory

Regulators like FINRA, the SEC, or state regulators, can examine an advisor and find they have violated a rule or law and require the advisor to disclose the violation. They can range from relative benign violations, like not keeping certain records, to very significant violations, like theft or insider trading.

3. Employer

An employer can affect a disclosure event when an advisor violates a company compliance rule, or any other rule or law. For example, if an advisor signs a client agreement instead of the client signing, that is forgery, which is illegal and not allowed by any regulators and—one would assume—against all corporate compliance departments. This usually gets an advisor fired and stays on the advisor's record forever.

4. Personal

Bankruptcies, misdemeanors, felonies, and other personal negative events can be shown in an advisor's disclosures. When you see these, apply common sense in evaluating them. For example, if an advisor was forced into bankruptcy due to uncovered medical expenses for a child or spouse's life-threatening condition and there are no other disclosures, this may not automatically preclude you from working with this advisor.

However, as a different example, if you see four misdemeanors in the recent past for driving while intoxicated (DWI) charges, clearly this advisor has personal control and judgement issues and you should find a different advisor to work with.

3. Check the website

First, an advisor should have a website or webpage on their employer's main website. If they do not, that is a red flag and you should proceed with caution in evaluating the advisor.

These days, given the highly regulated industry that financial advisors are in, most of their websites are standardized to a degree, scrutinized by their firm's compliance officers and, frankly, somewhat boring and generic due to the enormous regulatory burden they are put under that regulates their advertising.

What should be red flags on a website are statements that tout investment performance, guarantees, or individual client testimonials, the latter which are essentially outlawed—with some exceptions, notably someone who is only licensed to sell insurance, like fixed life insurance or health insurance. If your advisor has any such statements on their website, proceed with caution. If and when you speak with this advisor on the phone, ask them specifically about each of these items on the website and write down their answers. These specific questions are in the chapter on interviewing advisors.

4. Call the advisor on the phone

When you call an advisor for the first time (I do not recommend emailing an advisor for your first communication—you cannot learn as much in an email) simply tell the person who answers the phone or calls you back, "I am looking for a financial advisor; can you please tell me about your services?" Do not immediately tell them what you need, as a bad advisor may just mimic what you are saying. Force the advisor to tell you what they do for a living. To reiterate, there only a few high-level responses they can give you: they primarily invest money, they are a financial planner, they are a wealth manager (invest money and do financial plans), they are an insurance-focused advisor, or they focus on selling securities.

If a portion of their service is free, be very alert. For example, if an advisor does not charge for a financial plan and they sell investment products on commission, there could be an issue, especially if they have no professional, quality designations. Wealth management firms that both manage a portfolio and provide financial planning are fine if they do the planning for free, as they normally charge roughly 1 percent of your portfolio assets annually, and that can cover a full financial plan depending on your portfolio size. However, these firms almost always have a staff person that is credentialed to do the plan, so be aware if they do not.

In this first call, a huge red flag is any mention of specific products, rates of return, or guarantees. Keep in mind that despite what you see in movies like *The Wolf of Wall Street*, the days of very young, glib, fast-talking sales people are largely behind us. These days many advisors are actually not that terrific on the phone, so be patient with their explanation of what they do and who they are. However, if you feel like you got a character out of the movie *Wall Street* or *Boiler Room* on the phone, feel free to hang up on them. Believe me, if you are one of the few unlucky people to get this type of person on the phone, they are used to getting hung up on!

5. How much do they charge and how do they charge?

It is important to understand clearly what the advisor charges. A bad advisor will not be able to give you clear and specific answers. There are only a few ways for an advisor to charge for their services: a percentage of assets under management, in the 1 percent range normally; commissions on the sale of an investment or insurance product; hourly fees; a flat fee; monthly retainer; and, only in the case of a hedge fund for the high net worth investor, a percentage of the profit.

Advisors should be able to clearly give you exact figures for any of the ways they happen to charge. Some advisors will offer different way to pay them, and for each of the above methods, should be able to tell you near-exact figures over the phone.

For example, if you need life insurance because you just got married or had your first child, you should ask the advisor how much commission is being paid to the advisor and/or their firm. The advisor should have no problem telling you exactly how much commission he or she is getting on the sale of that product. In another example, if you need a financial plan, the planner should have no issue telling you what their hourly rate is and a rough estimate of the number of hours it should take based on your specifics. Of course, if you the client surprise the planner with brand new information after getting a quote, and more hours are needed, the planner should be able to articulate why the additional hours are necessary and you should understand this and not have a problem with the extra cost. As a final example, if you are buying a stock, bond, or mutual fund and a commission is being charged, the exact commission you are paying should be readily provided when you ask.

If you cannot get a clear answer on how and what the advisor will charge you, do not hire the advisor; they either are fitting my definition of bad or are unethical.

6. Meet the advisor in their office

When you are comfortable, meet the advisor in their office—if they are in close proximity, of course, and you are not hiring an advisor far away. Bring another adult with you always. Your spouse, friend, sibling, or parent will be a useful second set of eyes and ears for your meeting.

In the context of this chapter of ferreting out a bad advisor, when meeting in their office, keep in mind the odds are very low you are meeting one. This said, you do not want to be one of the 3 percent, so be alert for anything that gives you a bad "gut feeling."

To be fair, it is very difficult to spot a bad advisor during or after an office visit. I have been in hundreds of advisors' offices over the years, and the spectrum of environments runs the gamut of tiny advisors whose office is in their basement with oil tank in full view, to suburban strip mall offices with mediocre furniture, to high-floor tower offices in New York, Chicago, or San Francisco replete with the most stunning views and furnishings right from a movie. Whether the office is minimal, or it is adorned with numerous degrees and "Top Advisor" awards, just pay attention to your surroundings. At the end of your meeting with the advisor, if anything gives you a bad "gut feeling," do not move forward to hire the advisor. The odds are they are not bad, but rather you do not have chemistry, and going with one's gut almost always works best. There are many advisors to choose from, so there is no reason to settle for someone that sets off any negative thoughts in the back of your mind.

The most important thing to do when in an advisor's office is to diligently go through the questionnaire that is shown in chapter 14 and pay attention to how the advisor reacts to the questions. Much more on this in the next chapter.

7. Answering Questions

If an advisor does not fully answer questions to your satisfaction or tries to baffle you with BS and lots of industry jargon, you may be speaking with a bad advisor. At minimum you have an advisor that is a bad fit for you. Advising someone on their finances whether you are a billionaire, millionaire, middle income, or at the poverty level, is a serious endeavor. Any advisor should be patient and take their time to explain and answer questions to your satisfaction.

If you have a great many questions prior to hiring an advisor, it is appropriate for the advisor to charge you by the hour, if need be, to answer your questions (if they are, in fact, basic questions).

8. Common Tactics Used by Bad Advisors

In this section, I will share some of the ways you can tell you may be speaking with a bad advisor. At minimum the tactics below are unprofessional, and that advisor should be avoided. At worst, these red flags could indicate you are speaking with an outright crook.

THE TAKE-AWAY CLOSE

A very old, and bizarrely effective technique working to this day is the "Take-Away" close, used to pressure someone to buy something. You will hear something like, "I don't think I can accommodate you; I have too many clients." or "I don't think I can get you into this investment; it's exclusive and time is running out," or "I can only give you access to [x] dollars or [y] number of shares of this opportunity." This is basically a psychological ploy to appeal to the basic instinct of being allowed into an exclusive club. There are only two scenarios where this tactic is not actually BS. One, if the advisor genuinely cannot take any more clients, and in that scenario he or she will tell in in the first fifteen seconds of your call and try to get off the phone fast to get back to working on their current client base. They will not try to keep you on the phone with "pregnant pauses" or other such emotional tactics.

The second is in the case of a genuinely limited investment like an IPO, for example, where only a fixed number of shares are being offered or a private placement where only a certain amount of money is being raised. In both cases, there is sufficient legal documentation available that can be sent to an attorney to check out.

MY INVESTMENT MODEL IS PROPRIETARY AND CANNOT BE SHARED

Today's advisors are well aware that transparency is needed, and very well aware that in this post-Madoff world there is distrust, and most will bend over backwards to share how they invest. If an advisor is reticent to share how they decide what stock, bond, mutual fund, or ETF to invest in on your behalf, you should be on high alert. The advisor, to be fair, may have a proprietary formula, for example, to tell them when a stock in undervalued and a great time to buy, but that can be explained in plain English. Secrecy in general is something to be very dubious about.

WITH INVESTMENTS, NEVER WRITE A CHECK OUT TO YOUR ADVISOR

With investing, a check is never written out to your advisor. It is always written out to the firm which is the custodian of your assets. For example, for an advisor who is employed at Merrill Lynch, Morgan Stanley, UBS, Wells Fargo, the checks are made out to the firm. For advisors who are Registered Investment Advisers, they use an independent custodian like Charles Schwab, Fidelity, TD Ameritrade, or Pershing.

For advisors who work for Independent broker-dealers like Royal Alliance, Securities Service Network, or Securities America, checks are almost always written out to the independent clearing firm, which is like a bank that the broker-dealer firm uses to hold securities and cash. The two largest of the roughly twenty clearing firms are Pershing and Fidelity. When speaking with an advisor, ask the advisor who the custodian of the money is, and if you are not familiar with that firm, Google the firm and call the headquarters just to be sure the firm is in fact separate and apart from your advisor. The only case where a check is written to your advisor or his firm is for hourly or monthly planning fees, and if the advisor works for a FINRA-registered broker-dealer, the broker dealer must permit that activity, and the advisor will have no issue proving he or she is permitted to offer planning services apart from the broker-dealer.

SMALL FIRM, PROPRIETARY INVESTMENTS

A proprietary investment can take many forms, but often it is an investment partnership that the advisor has created himself and is the general partner of. It can be a hedge fund investing in public securities, it can be a real estate fund purchasing buildings, or it can be a venture fund investing in startups. Statistically, it is rare for an advisor to have such an investment vehicle. However, there are hundreds of legitimate advisors with such funds out of hundreds of thousands of advisors that exist. They are expensive to create, and here comes the major red flag: if the advisor is a small advisor in terms of assets under management (AUM), then something does not add up.

For example, I personally know of several very mature RIA firms that are fee-only wealth management companies that also have their own investment partnership. They are quite legitimate, and these partnerships are small in dollar amount relative to the firm's total AUM, which often exceeds a billion dollars. These firms can afford the high expense of auditors, accountants, bonding, and other costs to support this esoteric vehicle. Almost always, the RIA started the fund from client demand, in that the clients wanted to invest in an alternative asset that had the potential to provide greater returns over time. Those returns would be uncorrelated to the general stock markets.

For a small firm to have a proprietary product and less than, say, one hundred million dollars, there are very good odds something is wrong. There are always exceptions, but extraordinary care must be taken to vet this type of firm. In addition, if the advisor has an active FINRA license with a broker-dealer, then the red flag just got dramatically more alarming, as a FINRA BD would almost never allow their rep to create an outside investment product. Again, there are always exceptions, but tread very carefully when you encounter this scenario.

IS YOUR CURRENT ADVISOR BAD?

Mark Spangler was a Registered Investment Adviser, which by definition is a fiduciary. He was fee-only, meaning he had no broker-dealer affiliation and took no commissions. At one time he was the president of the only national fee-only adviser trade association, was on the cover of many trade association magazines, and spoke at many industry events. In fact, representing that trade association, he spoke for me once at a conference educating the audience on what it meant to be fee-only. I would occasionally bump into him at industry events, so what unfolded in future years were both shocking and a lesson.

In 2014 Mark Spangler was found guilty of thirty-two criminal counts of investment adviser fraud, wire fraud, and money laundering. He is currently serving a sixteen-year sentence. Spangler, it turned out, got "Tech Venture Fever" while operating an advisory firm in Seattle, Washington, watching all the Microsoft people and related investors make many millions on startups. It appears at some point, he decided to invest his clients' money in two tech firms instead of the typical securities he used to invest in—such as stocks, bonds, and mutual funds. One tiny problem: he never told his clients he was doing this. Moreover, he created entirely fake account statements to make it look like clients were still invested in standard securities. They had no idea their money was invested in just two privately held, high risk, private companies. It turned into a Ponzi scheme when clients wanted their money back and he decided to raise new money to pay back exiting investors. One of the companies collapsed entirely and investors lost fifty million dollars.

This was shocking to the industry on many levels. First, Mark was considered one of the early leaders in fee-only financial advice, and one of the last people you'd think would purposefully violate so many laws, given his advocacy to the opposite. Second, when meeting Mark, he was a little awkward socially. He was the opposite of a slick operator. He wore these ugly sweaters for his industry photo-ops, and perhaps this awkward persona is what threw people, myself included. Third, to outright fabricate client statements is so unbelievable, it's a Madoff-like level of fraud.

Spangler did commit Madoff-like fraud, albeit on a much smaller, less egregious scale. Because of the parallel, Paul Sullivan, *New York Times* columnist, has quoted me on how to avoid such a case. In one such conversation, Paul had asked me about Spangler. I shared with Paul that a few years prior to his arrest, I bumped into Spangler at a trade show. In casual conversation, Spangler shared that he no longer invested client money in standard securities like stocks, bond, and mutual funds; instead, he invested in privately held tech companies, as their investment returns were far greater. Our conversation in fact took place right in front of the exhibit booth of one of the companies he was a major investor in. I recall thinking how very unusual for an advisor to put all client money into private companies. I had never heard of any advisor doing this. I never thought about it again until I read about his fraud in the news.

From this experience, I learned three very important lessons that everyone should heed. First, just because someone says they are something—in Spangler's case, a fiduciary—does not mean it's true. These days, many people hear the word fiduciary and essentially stop their due diligence, which could be a tragic mistake.

Second, people can change, and when you see a change, you should stop and take notice. Third and most important, independently verify what your advisor tells you. In Spangler's case, his clients could have found out within ninety days that he was committing fraud and put a stop to it much sooner. They could not have prevented the fraud, but could have mitigated it.

If your current advisor is managing your portfolio or selling you securities, there is a fool-proof way to check if your money is there and in the securities you are shown or told they are in. This technique will work for any advisor regardless if they work for a giant like Merrill and the advisor is a commission-based advisor, or if the advisor is fee-only and your assets are custodied at a discount broker like Schwab.

Simply Google the name of the bank, broker, or custodian firm that is holding your cash and securities. Get the 800-number that shows up on your search engine. Make sure the same phone number for headquarters shows up on Google more than a couple times. Call that number and speak to someone in customer service and have them tell you what is in your account. Compare that to what your advisor has been sending you. They should match nearly identically, absent recent transactions, market fluctuations, and so forth. Do this every ninety days—forever. I literally mean forever. Never stop. Put it in your calendar. It's your money, and you do not want to be one of the small number of investors that gets taken in by a Madoff or Spangler.

To be crystal clear, for this to work perfectly, do not call any phone number the advisor gives you, nor rely upon what he or she sends you in print or electronically. The whole point is to cold call the main number of the custodian's headquarters and get your account validated. If your account is dramatically different, call your attorney and/or your local police department immediately.

CHAPTER 14

SCREEN TEST: INTERVIEWING ADVISORS

This chapter is perhaps the most important one for many readers. When meeting with potential financial advisors, it is vital to ask many questions, record their answers, then reflect on their answers and compare them to the other advisors' interviews you conduct. This process is also applicable to your current advisor relationship if you have one. In fact, one could argue that it is even more important to go through this process with your current advisor. It will give you a better understanding of your advisor, and in some cases, may lead you to find an advisor that is a better fit.

Before getting to the interview questions, I will share views and experiences of four different people that offer unique perspectives when evaluating an advisor. These experiences will help you think more expansively about the advisor you are interviewing and give you alternative points of view.

ADVICE ON GETTING ADVICE FROM A VETERAN

Don Trone has been helping advisors improve the quality of financial advice for more than three decades. Before he entered the financial services industry, he was helping others as a long-range search and rescue helicopter pilot in the U.S. Coast Guard. He shared with me that first responders always put first the needs of others. This basic but powerful ethos has been at the heart of all the work he has done.

Don went on to become the founding CEO of fi360, the first company to build a platform that integrates fiduciary tools with training and a professional designation. He also was the founding President of Foundation for Fiduciary Studies, which published the first industry handbook on fiduciary best practices.

His current firm, 3ethos, is conducting original research in the development of standards and training programs in the new fields of behavioral governance and neuro-governance. Behavioral governance is the study of the interrelationships between leadership, stewardship, and governance. Neuro-governance is the follow-on research that studies the neurological markers and psychological behaviors of exemplary leaders and stewards.

Don defines leadership as the capacity to inspire and engage others. Stewardship is the passion and discipline to protect the long-term interests of others. Governance is the ability to demonstrate the details of a prudent decision-making process.

He shared that the best way for a consumer/investor to determine whether they're working with the right advisor is to evaluate the advisor's leadership, stewardship, and governance:

1. If you're not inspired and engaged by your advisor, then your advisor is not a great leader.

2. If your advisor does not demonstrate passion and the discipline to protect your long-term interests, then your advisor is not a great steward.

3. And, if your advisor can't articulate the details of their decision-making process, then your advisor is not a great governor (decision-maker).

It's also important for consumers/investors to understand that regulators are not the answer. Regulators are merely going to define the minimum standard of care an advisor must meet in order to conduct business. Regulators may define fiduciary standards and call the standards the highest defined by law—but, the operative words are "by law." The highest standards of care are defined in terms of leadership, stewardship, and governance.

KNOWING YOUR ALTERNATIVES ABOUT ALTERNATIVES

If advice on a portfolio of securities is part of your need, there are many things that you should be asking of your advisor.

William J. Kelly (Bill) is the CEO of the Chartered Alternative Investment Analyst (CAIA) Association, a global leader in alternative investor education, founded in 2002. Its mission is to study alternatives and to administer its CAIA credential demonstrating competency and professionalism for financial advisors when they evaluate alternative investments for their clients. In its most simplistic description, an alternative investment is an investment vehicle that generally is different from and does not fluctuate in price at the same time as stocks and bonds. As the saying goes, its smart not to put all your eggs in one basket; put another way, you should diversify your investments. This concept becomes incredibly important if you are within fifteen years of retirement.

Bill has spent most of his thirty-year career in the asset management industry at firms big and small, in various roles from Chief Operating Officer to Chief Financial Officer to Chief Executive Officer. One very notable firm and role was as one of the founding partners at Boston Partners, which went from a startup in one of the founder's homes to fifteen billion dollars in assets under management by the time he left. It now manages one hundred billion dollars.

Alternatives in the past used to be available to only the very wealthy, with investments like Private Equity and Venture Capital having either very high minimum requirements or rules that only allowed the wealthy to invest. Times have changed and now alternatives are widely accessible in many forms, including the very popular Exchange Traded Fund structure. Because of the greater access and because of markets reaching new highs with signs of significant volatility, Bill believes the role of the financial advisor is more important than ever. The advisor needs to evaluate if alternatives are appropriate for an investor, and if so, which ones and to what degree.

As Bill shared with me, the global financial crisis of 2008 showed us that many investors took some kind of loss, then sat on the sidelines and watched and waited as the market came back. The lesson learned is to attempt to reduce an entire investment portfolio volatility and increase risk-adjusted returns; that is where alternatives can play a role, as they do not move in lockstep with the broader market in general.

The current challenge is financial advisors are now working hard to tell their clients that market highs won't last, they never do, and offsetting future corrections in the market is prudent. There are, however, forces making it harder for financial advisors to get this message across. There are myths and stigmas associated with alternatives, and journalists often use scary descriptors such as "risky" and "problematic" in their articles. Both the industry itself and the media can do a better job of educating the public.

Alternatives are still a relatively new industry, but a very serious one. In 2002 there were only forty-three candidates in the first class at CAIA, but now, over ten thousand hold the designation in ninety countries. The exam takes about four hundred hours to prepare for its two levels and is considered by many a complimentary designation to the Chartered Financial Analyst (CFA), one of the oldest designations in the industry. CAIA also offers a more approachable certificate-based program (Fundamentals of Alternative Investments), which is directed more toward the financial advisor community. Advisors can and should discuss alternative investments with their clients to see if and how they can benefit the investor and their goals.

ONE QUESTION CAN MAKE ALL THE DIFFERENCE

Sophia (not her real name) is in her forties, divorced, and has two girls both in their twenties. She is a unique investor because for over fifteen years she has worked at a consulting firm that serves all types of financial advisory firms, from the Wall Street giants to small advisory firms. She is a more knowledgeable investor than most.

Sophia takes a pragmatic approach to her wealth management. Now that her children's college needs are satisfied, her primary goal is securing her retirement. She regularly entertains proposals from other advisors to compare and contrast what others recommend to her current plan. She uses the same advisor that she chose for her and her ex-husband years ago. The advisor was referred to her by their accountant, and she was smart to ask if the CPA received any compensation from the advisor for referrals. He did not; he simply likes to refer to this particular advisor. For those that do, this practice is legal, and called a solicitor's agreement, and the fees must be fully disclosed to the client. This practice is not a bad practice per se, but for Sophia, she preferred to take no risks at all for this type of conflict, so she hired the advisor and uses him to this day. He has delivered acceptable performance, been responsive and communicative.

In searching for and working with an advisor, Sophia has very direct advice for anyone, but especially for women:

"If they are in any way condescending, patronizing, simply walk away. Your advisor must be willing to answer any and all questions, freely give you all costs involved so you know exactly what you are paying. It is your money, and you should treat this service like any major buying decisions such as a house, or car. Do a ton of research and be prepared. Know yourself and your needs, preferably prior to meeting with an advisor. Be comfortable to put your potential advisor on the spot by asking hard questions. If he or she has a tough time answering these hard questions, do not hire them."

A terrific lesson for all comes from an experience Sophia recently had. She received a phone call from an advisor affiliated with her bank requesting a meeting to review her retirement investments. She agreed, and after a meeting, he began to write up a proposal. While she was waiting for his proposal, Sophia looked up this advisor's background on the www.Finra.org website, the regulator that provides free access to advisors' backgrounds. Sophia learned that this advisor was only employed part-time at the bank; the other half of his work week was spent working at a restaurant. Sophia shared with me that so few investors actually look up their advisor. While a very small percentage of advisors are part-time, one certainly does not want to be in the position of being surprised to learn of an advisor's background that makes you uncomfortable after it is too late.

Sophia did not switch to him for a number of reasons, including his youth and part-time status, but mostly due to his overly aggressive manner and having overly ambitious projections for her portfolio.

GOOGLE IS YOUR BEST FRIEND

Sameer Somal is the CFO of Blue Ocean Global Technology and also holds the CFA, CAIA, and CFP designations. He considers himself both a passionate learner and educator. He frequently lectures at financial services industry events on the digital revolution, on reputation management, and provides continuing education classes to CFPs, CPAs, attorneys, as well as being a subject matter expert witness for law firms in cases involving online reputation. He currently serves on CFP Board's Council on Education and the CFA Institute FAS Board of Regents, and hosts the CFAI talk show, "The Topic @ Hand."

His company works with advisors and their firms to ensure their digital presence represents their actual expertise. All too often, an advisor can have deep expertise in a client niche or investment strategy, yet if that expertise is not seen online, a consumer may simply not even be aware that advisor's expertise exists. Sameer stated that every second, sixty-three thousand searches are done on Google. Given that reputation is everything in business, especially in the financial advice business, it is critical for consumers to evaluate the information found online to help determine if a particular advisor is ideal for them. As much as online information can be used to find the right advisor, it can be used, and is most often used to eliminate someone from consideration.

Sameer explained to me some of the tactics that anyone can use to evaluate an advisor's online persona to help determine if they are ideal for you. He offered the Albert Einstein quote as way to open the examination of online personas: "Whoever is careless with truth in small matters cannot be trusted with important matters." When researching an advisor, an advisor that has demonstrated thought leadership on a particular topic by writing for trade journals, or a blog, or speaking at non-profits, can often illustrate someone who is committed to their trade...versus someone who has not. To be clear, the absence of these obvious public events does not in and of themselves mean anything negative. Rather, the presence of such public history allows you, the investor, to better understand this advisor.

When noticing things online about an advisor, carefully review his or her profile on LinkedIn, Facebook, Twitter, and the advisor's own website. Are there typos? Is there dated information, such as blog post from three years ago, but nothing more recent? These can be indictors of a lack of attention to detail or commitment. It could be the advisor is simply checking a box of something they read once they should do, but do not really believe in. You want an advisor that is true to him or herself, as that person will be more committed to you as a client. Of course, always check the FINRA site of www.brokercheck.org and related www. SEC.gov site to see if there is negative information. Another resource to consider is CFP Board's historical record of individuals disciplined by state: https://www. cfp.net/about-cfp-board/ethics-enforcement/disciplined-individuals-by-state. In summary, there are now a number of resources that let a consumer better examine a potential or current advisor using online information.

INTERVIEW QUESTIONS

This interview question section is broken down into two parts. The first part is for those who need financial planning help or a specific issue addressed. These questions are equally applicable for those who just need a plan and no asset management, those who need a plan and asset management (Wealth Management), or those who need one specific task that is a component of planning, such as college funding.

The second part is for those that need asset management, regardless if some planning is needed or not. Please note that the interview questions presume you read and followed chapter 12 on how to create your list of advisors, and chapter 13 on how to avoid a "bad" advisor.

I offer explanations and details in parenthesis along with many of the questions to give context. Make sure you ask these questions first and get your answers before you allow the advisor to ask you questions. This point is very important.

If the advisor insists on asking you questions first, that's a red flag the advisor is either hiding something or will try to map his answers to mimic your inquiry, or his client service skills are lacking.

All of these questions can be downloaded from the book website for your convenience: www.nicholasstuller.com

Print these questions out and bring one set to each of your advisor meetings. Ideally you want to meet with at least five advisors. After you have conducted all your face to face meetings, you will want to compare the answers on both an absolute and relative basis using the guide tips that follow after each question. To be very clear, do not give these forms to the advisor. Ask them the questions, and you complete the forms. It puts them on the spot and forces them to explain and you to write down the answers. This way, the odds are best you will understand fully the advisor.

PLANNER QUESTIONS

1. How long have you been doing financial planning? _____

2. How many financial plans have you done in your career? _____

3. How many financial plans have you done in the last twelve months? _____

4. What certifications do you have to illustrate competency? _____

5. When did you get these certifications? _____

6. If you do not have any certifications for financial planning, please explain how you can prove to me your competency and why you never acquired a professional designation.

_____

_____

_____

_____

(It is theoretically possible to have competency as a financial planner with no professional designations, however, it will be challenging to prove it.)

7. How do you stay educated and current with all the changes in this industry?

_____

_____

_____

_____

(Advisors have many resources to stay on top of their profession, from formal continuing education that is mandated by their certification body, to the employer having mandated education, to reading trade journals, to trade events, to something called a "study group" where advisors gather several times a year to learn from each other. You want to hear some kind of formal ongoing education process from the advisor.)

8. Have any of your certification bodies disciplined you for any reason? If yes, please explain the details.

_____

_____

_____

_____

9. In the last year, what are some of the more important developments in the industry that effects financial planning?

_____

_____

_____

_____

("Taxes" is too easy a reply, demand more developments than this. When you get home, research the terms/developments they gave you to understand their view on changes in the industry.)

10. What types of clients do you have?

_____

_____

(By age, income, profession, marital status, or other niche. It's ideal if your advisor has knowledge about where you are in life, or anything that will help the advisor understand and have an affinity for you as a person.)

11. Why did you become a financial planner?

_____

_____

_____

_____

(This question allows you to learn what motivates this person, and how much passion he or she has for the planning process. The true relative passion for financial planning will become clear as you compare the answers you receive from competing advisors. All else being equal, you want to hire someone who truly loves the planning process.)

12. If the advisor is a registered investment adviser (RIA): When was the last time you were examined by your state or the SEC?_____

Did you receive a Deficiency Letter?_____If yes, can you provide me with a copy?

_____

(Many RIAs have never been examined by their state or SEC, so don't be surprised if they have not been examined. If they have been visited, they almost always get a Deficiency Letter or some kind of written communication after the examination. It is standard practice in that a regulator has to justify the trip and write up the advisor for something. Keep in mind, an SEC or State examiner is simply giving an opinion as to whether the advisor is following its rules; it is not a legal opinion. Many advisors do not agree with the Deficiency Letter and formally reply to the Deficiency Letter, so ask for a copy of that as well. Asking for this reveals how comfortable the advisor is with being asked tough questions, and if he refuses to share the deficiency letter if he has one, it's a big red flag. The advisor should be fine with sharing it, and feel free to explain you understand most of them are benign. If the advisor wants to provide you a summary and not the actual letters, then that can be acceptable as well.)

13. If the advisor is a registered rep of a broker-dealer:
    a. Please share what limitations your broker-dealer might place on you.

_____

_____

(Every BD has different rules on what they allow their advisors to offer. For example, a BD may not allow their advisors to recommend viatical settlements, which allow you to sell a life insurance policy in the open market.)

b. Please share exactly how you will get paid, and estimate how much money you will make from me.

_____

_____

c. How can you assure me that the advice or product you are providing is in my best interests, as opposed to potentially compensating you the highest?

_____

_____

d. Are you also a fiduciary of an RIA? _____

e. On what occasions will you be fiduciary, and what occasions will you not be?

_____

_____

(A fiduciary is someone who puts the needs of the client ahead of his own. For example, this may mean the advisor makes less money in order to do the right thing for you. This is opposed to the suitability standard that brokers have, a lesser legal standard. The confusion is if the person is both an RIA and a broker, that person theoretically can sometimes act in your best interest and other times not.)

f. If you are never operating under a fiduciary standard, what assurance can you provide that you will put my interests above yours?

_____

_____

g. If your broker-dealer has a policy that does not allow you to put into writing that my interests are above yours, what is the pragmatic reason for this?

_____

_____

14. How do you charge for a financial plan? _____

If hourly, what is your rate? _____

If bundled in an Assets Under Management fee, what is your asset minimum to receive the plan as part of the engagement?_____

If a monthly retainer fee, what is the usual fee? _____

If paid via commissions, please explain exactly how that would work—what products and what would those commission costs be? _____

_____

15. If you have any FINRA or SEC/State disclosures, please explain what happened.

_____

_____

_____

_____

16. Every advisor has a potential conflict of interest, what are yours?

_____

_____

_____

_____

17. What information do you need from me in order to create my plan?

_____

_____

_____

_____

(It should be a fair amount of information they need about you, family, earnings, savings, taxes, homes, health issues, and the like.)

18. What questions do you have for me? (List out every question they ask of you!)

_____

_____

_____

_____

19. Finally, based on my answers, what do you think it would cost to create my plan?

_____

20. Do you, or does your firm, have E&O (Errors and Omissions) Insurance? If yes, please provide information on the coverage. _____

Asset Manager Questions

21. How long have you been doing Management? _____

22. How many clients are you managing money for? _____

23. What is your typical account size? _____

24. Who is your Custodian or Clearing firm(s)? _____

25. Do you manage portfolios yourself or do you select other managers? Please explain your process. _____

_____

_____

_____

_____

(In an earlier chapter a person that selects other managers is called an "Asset Gatherer," which is industry jargon for someone who believes that managing money should be done by others, and the advisor decides which other asset managers to use or not use. It's a philosophical belief, neither good nor bad, just different from other advisors who pick individual stocks or funds themselves.)

26. If you manage portfolios yourself, do you use a selection of individual stocks and bonds, or Mutual Funds or ETFs? Why? Do you make the trades without calling first? (discretion versus non-discretion) Please share some of the names of the securities you invest in._____

_____

_____

_____

_____

(Again, there is no right or wrong answer to this question. Often, the larger the investment portfolio—over two million dollars—the more likely an advisor will use individual stock and bonds, as many feel there are tax advantages and opportunity to achieve higher returns. Alternatively, some advisors use other money managers, called Separate Accounts. For portfolios under two million dollars, very often portfolios of mutual funds and ETFs are used, especially for a wealth manager, as he is doing a financial plan. Most planners use mutual funds as there is a focus on all the planning aspects, and not on monitoring the markets daily. On the topic of trading discretion, most fee-only RIAs use trading discretion—it's common. If the advisor is also a broker-dealer rep, more caution needs to be applied.)

27. What certifications do you have to illustrate competency? _____

28. When did you get these certifications? _____

29. If you do not have any certifications for asset management, please explain how you can prove to me your competency and why you never acquired a professional designation. _____

_____

_____

_____

_____

(There are a number of advisors who manage money with no professional designations, however, they should be able to explain in great detail their experience.)

30. How do you stay educated and current with all the changes in this industry?

_____

_____

_____

_____

(Advisors have many resources to stay informed and up-to-date on the industry, from formal continuing education that is mandated by their certification body, to the employer having mandated education, to reading trade journals, to trade events, to something called a "study group" where advisors gather several times a year to learn from each other. You want to hear that the advisor participates in some kind of formal ongoing education process.)

31. Have any of your certification bodies disciplined you for any reason? If yes, please explain the details. _____

_____

_____

_____

_____

32. In the last year, what are some of the more important developments in the industry that effects asset management?

_____

_____

_____

_____

("Taxes" is too easy a reply; demand more developments than this. When you get home, research the terms/developments they gave you to understand their view on changes in the industry.)

33. What types of clients do you have?

_____

_____

_____

(By age, income, profession, marital status, or other niche. It's ideal if your advisor has knowledge about where you are in life, or anything that will help the advisor understand and have an affinity for you as a person.)

34. Why did you get into asset management? _____

_____

_____

_____

(This question allows you to understand the motivations of this person.)

35. If the advisor is a Registered Investment Adviser (RIA): When was the last time you were examined by your state or the SEC?_____

Did you receive a Deficiency Letter?_____If yes, can you provide me with a copy?

_____

(Many RIAs have never been examined by their state or SEC, so don't be surprised if they have not been examined. If they have been visited, they almost always get a Deficiency letter or some kind of communication, it's standard practice in that a regulator has to justify the trip and write up the advisor for something. Keep in mind, an SEC or State examiner is simply giving and opinion on whether the advisor is following their rules, it is not a legal opinion. Many advisors do not agree with the Deficiency letter and formally reply to the Deficiency letter, so ask for a copy of that as well. Asking for this reveals how comfortable the advisor is with being asked tough questions, and if they refuse to share the deficiency letter if he have one, it's a big red flag. They should be fine with sharing it, and feel free to explain you understand most of them are benign. If the advisor wants to provide you a summary and not the actual letters, then that can be acceptable as well.)

36. If the advisor is a registered rep of a broker-dealer:

a. Please share what limitations your broker-dealer might place on you:

_____

_____

_____

_____

(Every broker-dealer has its own rules on what the firm doesn't want its advisors to provide. For example, some BDs may not allow certain types of non-exchange traded real estate investments. Every firm is different, but it's good to know their limitations, and for certain, every BD does not offer every type of investment.)

b. How can you assure me that the securities you are providing are in my best interests, as opposed to potentially compensating you the highest?

_____

_____

c. Are you also a fiduciary of an RIA?_____

d. On what occasions will you be fiduciary and what occasions will you not be?

_____

_____

(If you are only having a portfolio managed, virtually all broker-dealers have an RIA as well, and the entire relationship is normally under the fiduciary standard. If not, ask more questions as to why not, as this is unusual.)

e. If you are never operating under a fiduciary standard, what assurance can you provide that you will put by interests above yours?

_____

f. If your broker-dealer has a policy that does not allow you to put into writing that my interests are above yours, what is the pragmatic reason for this?

_____

_____

37. How do you charge for managing a portfolio? What is the total cost of the portfolio—your cost, plus the cost of the underlying securities, including fund 12b-1 fees and others?

_____

_____

_____

(If paid in some way other than charging a percentage of assets under management, this is highly unusual; therefore, have them share exactly how that would work. If the total fees exceed 3 percent, this can be regarded as out of the norm.)

_____

_____

38. I am aware accurately predicting future returns is not possible, but what rate of return ranges should I expect? What industry benchmarks do you compare client portfolios to?

_____

_____

(Any projections or past performance need to be carefully scrutinized. For example, is the advisor's past performance audited by a third-party using standards such as GIPS? Is the advisor providing you model performance, and is the type and account size the same as yours? If being provided back-tested performance, be aware this is the least reliable. Make sure the advisor explains in plain English all the disclosures related to investment performance. If the advisor is predicting returns higher than historical returns of the last ten years, this is a potential red flag and pay close attention.)

39. Every advisor has a potential conflict of interest, what are yours?

_____

_____

_____

_____

40. Do you have any FINRA or SEC/State disclosures? If so, please explain what happened.

_____

_____

_____

41. What information do you need from me in order to begin managing my portfolio?

_____

_____

_____

(At minimum, the advisor should have you complete an Investment Policy Statement (IPS), which maps out your goals and what your advisor can and cannot invest in, as well as a risk questionnaire to understand how risk averse or not you are.)

42. What questions do you have for me? (List out every question they ask of you!)

_____

_____

_____

_____

43. Do you or does your firm have E&O (Errors and Omissions) Insurance? If yes, please provide information on the coverage. _____

EVALUATING THE ANSWERS IN AN ABSOLUTE AND RELATIVE MANNER

Some of these questions are very easy for the advisors to answer. Some of them, such as asking an RIA for a Deficiency Letter, if the advisor ever got one from a regulator, will likely unnerve the advisor. This is okay, since you want to observe how advisors answer difficult questions. Moreover, it is your money and future, and any question—as long as it is germane, polite, and objective—is fair to ask.

Absolute Wrong Answers

All the questions posed are ones that any advisor can answer, so if an advisor refuses to answer any of these questions, that is not a good sign. If an advisor tells you he has no conflicts, that too is a bad answer, since every advisor has some kind of conflict. If the advisor asks very few or no questions about your plan or managing your portfolio, something is amiss.

Bad Advice

Is it possible that after spending five or six full hours or more on the process of sourcing, narrowing, interviewing, then finally selecting an advisor, that your newfound advisor—a seemingly good match—can still give you bad advice? Unfortunately, yes. It is possible that the advisor could select a mutual fund that has horrible performance and your money is lost. It is possible that a recommended insurance policy has a clause that your new advisor missed that impacts you. It is possible that your brand new financial plan did not take into account a tax ramification unique to your state.

Many advisors and their firms have Errors and Omissions insurance in case of a mistake, which is very costly to you but can be helpful in the extreme cases. However, the way to minimize the odds of receiving bad advice in the first place is to select an advisor who offers you clear and demonstrable answers to all your questions on the forms I've provided. Especially important are answers about the advisors' investment methodologies, their experience, their credentials, if they are and are not a fiduciary, their total compensation, and the like. When comparing five completed interview questionnaires, it is usually very clear which advisor you shouldn't hire and who you should seriously consider based on clear answers, candor, written follow-up, and supporting documentation.

Comparing Answers Relative to Each Other

1. In weighing which advisor is best for you, you generally want your advisor to have the greatest amount of experience. The exception is if you are very young or have a very simple need, then a younger advisor may actually be better for you because you will likely relate better, and the advisor's rates will be more modest (since they are newer to the industry).

2. You want an advisor who has clients similar to you in assets, income, and life stage.

3. You want your advisor to be the least conflicted.

4. You want an advisor who has the most relevant experience and/or designation. Refer to the Finra website http://www.finra.org/investors/professional-designations for information on designations. There are many designations, but you should at least have a passing familiarity with them.

5. You want an advisor with whom you have a connection.

6. You do want to pay the lowest price possible, but not at the expense of competency, experience, or relationship. Like any commercial relationship, you can always negotiate fees.

7. You want an advisor who loves what he does and isn't a "sales person" per se. You want someone who is a practitioner of the craft. On the topic of commissions, if an advisor is paid by commission, that is not a bad thing in a vacuum. It is, however, a potential conflict that someone who is fee-only does not have. Fee-only advisors can have their own unique conflicts too, although those who take commissions generally speaking have more opportunity for conflicts. To be clear, you should never select an advisor solely based on how he is compensated.

8. You want your advisor to be investing in securities that can be researched, and firms like Morningstar or Value Line have coverage and research on. Low priced stocks, i.e. "penny" stocks, more than 10 percent of a portfolio in private non-traded securities, or insurance products that are used as investments are red flags and need to be researched in greater detail.

9. If you do not understand what the advisor is investing in, and do not understand the advisor, do not use that advisor until you understand what he is doing.

10. If you have ever hired someone as an employee, look at these completed forms like résumés. Would you hire this person to work for you?

11. Ask for three references. Call and speak to them and ask why they like this advisor.

[CHAPTER 15:]

THE SECRET TO WORKING WITH ADVISORS

The only way to get the best from an advisor is to be honest. Never hide information you deem insignificant. The more the advisor knows about your lifestyle, the better he can help you achieve your goals. There is critical information advisors need to create a strategy that will deliver impressive results. In short, the more information you give an advisor, the better he'll serve you.

DON'T SMILE AND NOD: TERRIFIC SCHWAB TV AD

If you don't understand something your advisor says or is doing, speak up and ask the question. Do not fall prey to the "Smile and Nod" affliction that so many investors have with their advisors. This affliction is actually acute with highly successful and intelligent investors. You are only hurting yourself by remaining ignorant of a tactic your advisor is taking. Your advisor may assume that, by not asking questions, you understand. Always ask the question.

There is a terrific TV ad from brokerage firm Charles Schwab that illustrates this, although it's clear it's not the singular goal of the ad. It shows a seemingly successful couple in their late forties or early fifties in vignettes interacting with various people asking smart questions about landscaping, superfoods, child education, cell phones, company vendors, car purchases, and finally meeting with their financial advisor. In the first six vignettes, the couple asks intelligent questions. In the final scene, there is no hard-hitting questions, just the advisor saying to them, "I think we should put you into our new fund," and the couple looking at each other, then turning to the advisor and in unison saying, "Okay," with a slight shoulder shrug. It's a wonderful visual of what investors should not do.

DON'T ASSUME YOUR ADVISOR DOES EVERYTHING

Your advisor will perform the services that are outlined exactly in the engagement letter or contract you have signed with him. It may be obvious, but many investors assume that other services are included, or assume that their advisor will bring up topics or advice on anything that could be remotely related to the specific work contracted for. Every advisor has one or a few areas of focus and interest, but do not maintain expertise in every aspect of finances. The advisor either has team members who have other expertise or tap into an informal network of experts.

I have often heard investors say, "I would have thought my advisor would have told me about this or he should have known to alert me on that..." It is easy to make assumptions about financial matters, but the reality is, you should not assume the advisor is responsible for anything other than the explicit services hired. If something is not in the contract that you want the advisor to handle, ask the advisor.

POLITELY DEMAND GREAT SERVICE

Financial advice is a service business, and like all businesses, it is impacted by customer service. You have every right to demand great service, and if you do demand great service, you will get it in almost all cases. Great service will yield to better results for your portfolio, your financial plan, or your individual project.

There are advisors who have developed very specific service models. Some advisors will purposely return phone calls twenty-four hours later, never sooner, with no exceptions. Their rationale is that this strategy allows them to manage their time and train their clients to understand that there really are no emergencies that can't wait twenty-four hours. I have a very different opinion, but what is important is that your advisor has a service model that meets your definition of service. Both parties need to be pleased with working with each other, but if your definition of service is drastically different than your advisor, that could be an issue.

OVERSHARING IS FINE

Almost everyone I've discussed this book with agrees that the level of effective communication between most investors and their advisors leaves much to be desired. Consequently, you as the client should share as much information and views as you can with your advisor concerning your wishes and dreams, fears, interests, and experiences. Please note I did not have the word "financial" placed in front of the word "wishes" in the preceding sentence.

Your wishes and dreams in life can be affected by all things financial, so it is in your self-interest to ensure that your hired financial professional is aware of what you want out of life. Then, by looking at your life goals, your advisor can help you achieve those life goals that happen to be impacted by the financial and wealth drivers, such as insurance, investments, taxes, and so forth.

If you have ever said to yourself "I have always wanted to...." you should absolutely finish that sentence and share it with your advisor. There is no guarantee that your advisor can magically make your wish come true, but if you never discuss it, the odds of achieving it are even less.

OPEN AND REVIEW YOUR STATEMENTS ASAP

If you paid for a financial plan, read that plan cover to cover and implement the entirely of the plan as soon as possible. It is amazing that so many consumers pay for a financial plan and don't implement it, which is a waste of money. But more critically, the component of the plan to accomplish a task will never get gone, and the cost of that could dwarf the cost of the plan itself. Follow the advice of the expert you hired! One of the advisors I interviewed for this book stated proudly that 80 percent of the specific tasks in the plans she draws up for her clients get implemented, and that is up from 60 percent a few years ago due to better processes. As a client of advice, I believe you should be implementing near 100 percent of your advisor's guidance, unless you have personally proven your advisor wrong on something, which, of course, is possible.

If you are having a portfolio managed you will get either one or two statements, no less frequently than once every ninety days. One statement will come from your brokerage account where the securities and cash are "stored." The other will come from your advisor, if the advisor works separately from your brokerage firm. In both cases, open the statements the day you get them. Do not let them accumulate. It is unlikely, but if something is wrong, you want to find out immediately. Do not forget the very important advice from chapter 13, about cold-calling your advisor's custodian every ninety days to confirm that your funds are in your account and match the amounts on your statements.

For most everyone else, however, you want to see how your investments are doing. You want to be connected and involved in the process. You want to understand, for example, why your advisor sold Tesla stock and bought GM stock, as just one theoretical example. In wealth management, ignorance is not bliss. It's financial suicide. Its tantamount to your physician saying, "Do the following to improve your health," and you completely ignore him. It's simply not smart and a waste of time and money.

COMMUNICATE REGULARLY

You should speak with your advisor at least once per quarter. You should chat for no less than five minutes, and no longer than fifteen minutes, absent some specific issue that takes longer. The reason for this is after the one to two minutes of pleasantries, your work together will come up, and the likely "everything is fine" statement will come out of your mouth. By staying on the phone for up to fifteen minutes, both of you will probably think of something you've been meaning to ask the other that is meaningful for your portfolio or financial life. It might be a question you've had about a bond or interest rates. The advisor may have a question for you because of something you said. Good things come from developing and deepening a relationship and that only comes after spending a little time together.

CHECK THE ADVISOR'S REGULATORY RECORD EVERY NINETY DAYS

I stressed this in chapters 12 and 13, but it's worth repeating here. Check out your advisor's regulatory record on either the FINRA or SEC site. For this chapter, however, do it every ninety days. This may seem a little overkill, but what if three clients in the span of the last sixty days accused your advisor of wrongdoing? Don't you think you'd want to know this? Would you rather know this now or later? If you see something on his record, call the advisor and ask for an explanation. To reiterate, the odds are less than 7 percent that your advisor will ever have something appear, but it's better to know sooner, than not know at all.

FORMAL ANNUAL REVIEWS

If your advisor does not have formal annual reviews of your portfolio/plan, you should insist on it. Comparing investment returns to the indexes, evaluating actual portfolio costs, re-taking investment risk profile tests, reviewing personal changes in your life, and looking at retirement projections, are all things that should be done once per year. The review should result in a written report from your advisor of how things are going.

DO NOT ASSUME YOUR ADVISOR IS "RIPPING YOU OFF"

"Trust but Verify" was attributed to Ronald Reagan as it applied to the Russians. If you followed the guidance from chapter 13 on avoiding a "bad" advisor and used the advice in chapter 14 on interviewing an advisor, you will not need to fear your advisor taking advantage of you. However, many investors do not open up to their advisors due to lack of full trust, and that can be a mistake.

If you still have doubts about your current advisor, you can always spend a few hundred dollars to have another wealth manager give you a second opinion on what is being done for you, and you'll be able to sleep better and open up more to your advisor. Just as you wouldn't think twice about getting a second or even third medical opinion, you should take a similar approach with your advisor. Second guess the person to be certain everything is going as it should be.

GIVING REFERRALS

The best way to get outrageously wonderful results and service from your advisor is to help send the advisor new clients. During your first meeting with an advisor, you should tell the person outright that you have several friends who need an advisor and if your relationship works well, you'll be happy to make introductions. Of course, if you have absorbed the basics of this book, statistically, not all the people you refer to the advisor should hire that advisor, and that advisor should not take all your referrals. But, if you are genuine in your desire to send new clients to this advisor, the advisor will bend over backwards for you. You may think you don't know anyone to refer. Actually, you do. Less than half of all American adults have an advisor, so less than half your friends have an advisor. If you start discussing advisory relationships with friends, you collectively will learn more and be better consumers of advice, which will benefit your wealth goals.

Why should you be genuine about this? Because you will be performing a service for your friends who need professional financial help. You are doing a good thing. A person always feels better when he or she helps someone, so why not?

Advisors, more so than most other professions and businesses, highly value referrals. The brutal truth of this is that most financial advisors are not great business people. Between laws and regulations that control—or even forbid—certain marketing activities, to advisors' time being dominated by staying on top of changes in the industry, advisors are generally not good marketers. Therefore, referrals are more highly valued by advisors than almost any other business person. In fact, you may not realize that it is illegal for financial advisors to use a named client testimonial in an advertisement or on a website. Imagine if you are a plumber, or a make a piece of software, or run a restaurant, and you can't use your own clients as testimonials in ads? It may be crazy indeed, but it is one of the many rules that govern financial advisors and make it so hard to market an advisory practice. Therefore, referrals are highly valued.

Use the fact that you can be very helpful to the advisor's growth as a genuine driver to get the best possible relationship and results. On the flip side, advisors know full well that if you are unhappy, you are likely to tell ten times more people about the bad experience, so that is a valuable driver for your benefit as well.

SPOUSAL DIFFERENCES

If you are married or have a partner, it is vital to communicate to your advisor how the two of you differ in opinion. No partners have identical views on anything, and that is especially true when it comes to money and investing. Marriage counselors, divorce attorneys, the clergy, and surveys have shown us all that money is one of the leading drivers to relationship discord.

Imagine being in the office of your advisor and bickering in front of him over investment styles. "Active funds are the way to go," says the wife. "Passive funds are a much better bet over the long haul," says the husband. As you can imagine, your advisor will be spending time playing referee, working hard not to offend either of you. The problem with that is, if your advisor is working hard as an amateur marriage counselor, she is not spending time on your investments, plan, or problem you hired her to address in the first place.

It is inevitable that every advisor plays referee at some point in time. However, it pays to lessen that chance by being as prepared as a couple as best you can. Here are some things you should consider doing prior to your next meeting with your advisor:

1. Make sure you each know exactly what investments, insurance policies, savings accounts, and credits cards you each have separately and as a couple. Believe me, I have seen many people married for decades who don't know what accounts their spouses have.

2. Discuss your personal investment philosophies together to make sure you each understand the other's views. You don't want to be surprised about the other's views in the advisor's office.

3. If you have children, discuss what your plans are for their education and inheritance. The sooner your advisor has a unified view, the sooner she can help you achieve your goals.

4. Get all documents out and ready to show your advisor. This can take some time, especially if each of you has been handling different responsibilities. Start digging into your files two weeks prior to your next advisor meeting.

5. Discuss life expectancy and quality of life issues, should something happen to the other unexpectedly. No one likes to discuss end-of-life issues, but this is an important subject for your advisor.

GETTING PROFESSIONAL REFERRALS

Most advisors have networks of CPAs, attorneys, and other professionals to connect whenever you need to consult with certain experts. When you need a complimentary professional, it is wise to leverage the existing relationship you have with your financial advisor by asking for a professional referral. The additional virtue is if there are issues you have both financial advice and legal implications—for example, creating or updating a will—then the two professionals who already have a working relationship will not only yield a better result for you, but will likely result in you paying a lower fee.

SETTING UP YOUR CHILDREN, SIBLINGS, AND OTHERS

If you are satisfied with your advisor, you should get your family involved with finding and hiring a financial advisor as well. You do not necessarily need to refer your immediate family to your advisor, and you may not want to for privacy or other reasons. However, by helping your family members find an ideal advisor for them, you will have this important subject matter in common, and over time, discuss and debate various issues surrounding the use of your advisor. The output of this dialog will likely give you an edge in optimizing your advisor relationship by asking smarter questions, and in turn your advisor will likely perform better for you knowing you are an educated consumer of financial advice.

If you own or manage a business, there is a significant amount of innovation around workplace benefits, largely from technology companies. Helping employees get professional advice is now a benefit at many companies. Senior executives for decades have received financial advice as part of their compensation packages, but now with the combination of technology and the greater awareness of advisors serving consumers at all levels, it could be a very smart strategy to help your employees get personal financial advice.

DON'T LET SOCIAL MEDIA AND SPEED OVERTAKE UNDERSTANDING

Speed, social media, competition for attention, and everyday stresses have been pulling people into spending less and less time learning about the subjects they should focus on. Apps on our iPhones seduce us, claiming that everything from investing to dating can be accomplished with one swipe. This disturbing trend may be reversing itself. Even Twitter expanded the number of characters it allows users to use in postings. My point is that one of today's most successful and widely used applications has stated that we need more space, and by extension, more time to express ourselves.

That lesson needs to be extrapolated to other endeavors, but definitely to the smart use of your financial advisor. Slow down and take time to engage with your advisor. Peter Lynch, the famed portfolio manager of the incredibly well-performing Fidelity Magellan fund, was often quoted as saying, "Investors spend more time planning their vacations than they do on their retirements." This is still true to this day, but you can reverse that trend with your advisor, whether your goal is a secure retirement, your parent's well-being later in life, or starting that non-profit you always wanted to.

BE COMFORTABLE CHALLENGING YOUR ADVISOR

If you do not agree with your advisor about her recommendations, you should always feel free to disagree and discuss the proposed approach. Your advisory relationship is just like every other relationship in life; there will be periods of disagreement. Sometimes you will be correct and sometimes you won't. The point is to very quickly speak up about something with which you are not comfortable with and get to the bottom of the issue.

Think of it like having a contractor in your home. If you see something that appears odd or makes you uncomfortable with, speak up.

CHAPTER 16

ARE YOU SURE YOUR CURRENT FINANCIAL ADVISOR IS APPROPRIATE FOR YOU?

When you have a high fever or a painful sore throat, you visit your family physician. You don't go to an ophthalmologist, chiropractor, or chiropodist. Clients need to understand what their financial advisors do, why they picked them, and have realistic expectations about outcomes.

But don't beat yourself up if you picked the wrong financial advisor. Self-flagellation won't get you anywhere. If it makes you feel better, and it probably won't, you're not alone. You have plenty of company to console you.

But the public is not entirely to blame. Wall Street, the media, regulators, and the financial services industry had a great deal to do with it. If you currently have a financial advisor, there is some chance you may have the incorrect one. In this chapter we will explore how this could have happened, the signs that you have the wrong advisor, and what to do about it.

There is a rather obvious reason why there is a mismatch between the advisor and investor, and that is when your advisor is clearly doing the wrong thing for you via malfeasance, fraud, theft, and the like. The vast majority of advisors do the right thing for their clients; however, you need to ensure your advisor is not one of the small percentage who are doing wrong. This is such an important topic that I have devoted an entire chapter to the topic on spotting and avoiding a bad advisor. For the purposes of this chapter, I am assuming your current advisor is not involved in malice, misdeeds, fraud, or theft.

There are four reasons why you could have the wrong financial advisor. First, you could have originally selected the wrong advisor. If this turns out to be the case, don't feel too bad, as it is more common than you think. Consumers don't know what they don't know, and did the best they could with the information they had at the time they selected their advisor.

Second, the advisor could have made a mistake taking you as a client. Every client is not right for every advisor. For example, there can be a mismatch when it comes to needs versus the expertise the advisor has. A simple case can be that a consumer has inherited a significant stock portfolio, and is unsure what to do with it. A financial advisor who only creates financial plans but does not perform investment management services with regularity should not take this person as a client, unless the consumer needs a financial plan. Someone who manages assets is needed to examine the investment aspects as well as the tax implications of an inherited portfolio.

There are only two reasons why an advisor mistakenly takes you as a client. One, the advisor made an honest mistake, which will happen from time to time. We are all human and mistakes will happen. Correcting the mistake quickly is vital. Second, the advisor took you as a client regardless of fit, which only happens out of greed. I will show you how to find out if this is the case later in this chapter.

The third reason for having the wrong advisor is something in your life changed and your advisor is no longer a good fit for you. I will give you a re-al-world example. I know of someone in the arts whose income dropped dramatically in recent years. He has had the same advisor for years, and still pays the same percentage fees on his investment account. He stopped making contributions to his retirement accounts. He needs to change advisors because he no longer can afford the one he has. In fact, the real advice he needs now is budgeting and career advice to either increase his earnings or lower his costs, or ideally both. This investor knew the early warning signs of this negative income trend long before the advisor did and should have looked for a different advisor. To be fair, once the advisor saw the contributions dropping, he should have been on the phone with the client to uncover the issue. The bottom line is this mismatch was the fault of the consumer and he should have taken action.

The fourth reason for a client-advisor mismatch is something with your advisor has changed. For example, if your advisor is retiring soon or contemplating selling her firm, you need to understand the impact on you. In recent years because of the aging of the advisory world, firm owners seek to retire or are considering selling their firm. While this is a normal and expected eventuality, there is a way to sell an advisory firm that does not negatively impact the clients. If your advisor is retiring or selling, he or she should have years ago begun planning for who will take over managing the client relationships. The philosophies, service levels, and investment beliefs should all be aligned so that you as a client are seamlessly taken care of. The last thing you as a client want to hear is your advisor is retiring in a year or has sold his advisory practice. If you feel surprised or shocked and the transition is happening soon, that is a huge red flag, and seeking a new advisor is prudent.

I will give you another real-world example and one I saw up close. In the mid 1990s when I worked in the Advisor Division of Waterhouse Securities, now TD Ameritrade, I had an advisor client that made a philosophical shift in his firm's investment strategy. He decided to stop investing in individual stocks, and instead, invest his clients' money in open-ended mutual funds. At any point of time, this move is a dramatic investment shift, but was especially so at that time. Interestingly, it turns out many thousands of advisors made the same shift in the ensuing years.

Now, if you were a client of this advisor, perhaps you did not care, or maybe truly did not understand this shift. But if you personally believed in individual security holdings—loved your McDonald's stock, for example, because you had been going there since you were a kid and believe it's a great long-term investment because you are a loyal customer—your advisor's shift is meaningful. A few of his clients left him, which was the right thing for both parties. To stay with the relationship with such a difference in philosophy is unhealthy, and sooner or later, the relationship would end badly in all likelihood.

Any substantive change in your advisor's firm should be noted and carefully considered. For example, your advisor may be leaving a well-known firm to work at another firm. Is he leaving simply to increase his own compensation, or are there benefits to you, the client, as a result of the move? If your advisor has increased his account minimum, will your service begin to diminish? Has your advisor just created a new investment product that he is proposing you consider? These are all serious changes that need careful examination.

YOUR ADVISOR MAY NEED TO FIRE YOU

Regardless of the reason why your advisor is no longer a fit, one of you should make the decision to change. Sometimes the advisor will make the decision first, and that is fine, because he may realize the lack of a fit before you do. In fact, almost every advisor has a client or even several whom they truly want to fire. Many advisors never do it, but there are four reasons why an advisor should fire that client. For years I have worked with advisors who complain about clients but never terminate the relationship for one reason or another. Sometimes the advisor does not want to give up the revenue, but that is a horrible reason. There are cases where the advisor fears that word might get out and it could damage his or her reputation. While this fear is justifiable, it is negative short-term thinking. Still other advisors procrastinate and just don't want to deal with the angst of terminating a relationship, which again is not a professional way of dealing with the situation.

Interestingly, advisors feel pressure from industry consultants who state that advisors should focus on the best clients only, usually the largest, claiming profitability reasons. The odd reality is that there are not many studies that used real data tracking the true profitability of every single client an advisor has. As a service business, very few advisory firms using a time billing software system like a law firm or CPA, so there is no substantive empirical evidence or data to support firing a client based on profitability.

There is a very legitimate movement currently for advisors to focus on one or a couple of niches, so that the advisor can be more expert and provide a greater level or service. As I've mentioned previously, there are a great many niches, such as medical doctors, educators, or a particular investment strategy like covered call writing; therefore, if your advisor has decided to focus on a niche that you do not fit, that can be a reason to cease a relationship.

Regardless of the reason, if your advisor wants to terminate your relationship, then you are better off not working with the advisor and seeking an advisor who truly wants you as a client.

There are four justifiable reasons that warrant an advisor terminating a client relationship.

You do not take your advisor's critical advice. This is the big one, and a recent story from a friend hammered this home for me. My friend is the client who should be fired by his current advisor. My friend insists on investing in a certain type of security that gives him a very high level of income, but the risk to his principal is too high. His advisor has repeatedly told him he is gambling with his future, because of his age he cannot afford to risk his principal, but my friend does not listen. Note that I use the word *critical*—most clients don't take every piece of advice given, but the critical ones need to be followed.

The second reason to terminate a relationship is to protect you, the client. If an advisor has decided that you are not a fit, hopefully your next advisor will be a better fit and be better off. Call it karma, call it good will, whatever, but it's the right thing to do.

Thirdly, if the advisor and you genuinely do not have a good personal relationship at any level, you should be happy to be asked to move on. This sounds harsh, but if at every level the two of you do not get along, there is no sense to continue. Odds are very good a lot of the great advice you are receiving you are not implementing, as that is human nature, so we are back to the second reason to protect you, the client.

Fourth and finally, a reason for an advisor to terminate the relationship is to protect the advisor and the firm. In emotional times, especially with a market downturn, a client can unfairly blame the advisor and an attorney can fan these unfortunate flames. I have seen this first hand at brokerage firms and in the work I have done with advisors. There are even famous cases at discount brokers, where the client called in a trade to a call center, then later successfully sued for not being stopped after they lost money on the trade.

So, what should you expect if this happens to you? First, your advisor should be very frank and polite and simply state that for one of the above reasons, you should part ways and a different advisor will work better for you. The advisor should offer to refer you to other advisors and make an introduction and help with the transition. The advisor should be genuine in his concern for you and your future. For anyone in any business, be it a service or a product-based business, firing a client is a very hard thing to do. However, if the circumstances demand it, you as the client are truly better off.

"I HAVE MET THE ENEMY, AND IT IS ME"

I just wrote about a friend who ignores critical advice from his advisor. The situation is actually far worse that it seems because this friend of mine has a very tenuous financial situation. He has been ignoring his financial advisor for a very long time and has the distinct chance of outliving his money due to ignoring his hired professional's advice.

Can you envision ignoring a hired professional's advice in other areas? How about when your architect states you need a steel beam in that addition you are planning, but you say, "No, not necessary." The results could be devastating. Why do some people do this? This book cannot contemplate all the psychological reasons why some people defy the advice of trained professionals. However, I will attempt to illustrate why this happens and how to combat this urge if you happen to be someone who occasionally ignores great advice.

First, I have found that sometimes highly intelligent people can be myopic. They believe because they are highly skilled in one area, such as technology, law, or medicine, that naturally they should be similarly brilliant in all things wealth management. Sometimes this indeed is the case. Sometimes it is not, and they have a problem. They are blind to the fact that they are missing something, and often too late. For example, how did so many incredibly bright and successful

185

people get taken by Bernard Madoff? For some it was this malady of being so smart they thought they could not get taken to the cleaners. For others, it was ego, as they did not want to admit they did not know what due diligence questions to ask. Others were too lazy and depended literally on the word of others, who supposedly did their diligence. Finally, for others it was a failure of imagination, to envision that possibly this guy Bernie, a world-renowned investor, might be a scammer.

For my friend, being fired by his long-time advisor would be the best thing for him. I believe not only is his advisor doing him a massive disservice, but he is putting his firm in major legal liability by not firing him. If he indeed runs out of money, an attorney could make a decent case that the advisory firm knows better and should have saved him from himself. Of course, in reality, both parties are at fault. So, in my opinion, getting fired could be the best thing for my friend. If done gracefully, and backed up with some detailed reasons, this could be a wake-up call for him, and he could go into his next advisory relationship with a more balanced view to truly listening to someone whose life is dedicated to financial advice.

Over the years I have heard many stories from people about their financial advisors. In some cases, their advisor clearly seems to be doing the wrong things. In some cases, all seems well. Finally, I have heard the other stories where I am convinced the consumer is incorrect in his assessment. Again, I suggest you read chapter 13 on how to understand if you have or are about to hire an unscrupulous financial advisor. Now, I am focused on how you the client could have the wrong advisor, and you might be the issue.

At one brokerage house where I worked, for several months my desk was close to the recording system the firm had in place, which was in a large open-floor plan office. Most firms at that time, and to my understanding today, do not record all calls, but this firm did. On a weekly basis, the chief compliance officer of the firm would go to the very large reel-to-reel recording system and play back a conversation as he was investigating a client complaint. I would hear all sorts of complaints, ranging from the client saying the broker only bought one hundred shares of a stock when in fact he had asked for a thousand shares, to a conversation where the broker literally was saying something so unintelligent, he was removed from his position within days.

What I learned was this particular brokerage firm admitted quickly to any mistakes their employees made. Second, and this was the shocking revelation, that often the client made the mistake, but the real lesson for me was the client found it inconceivable that he had made the mistake—until, of course, the tape was played back. "No, Mr. Jones, you did not ask your broker to buy ten thousand shares of that stock that doubled in three weeks. You asked for one hundred shares. Shall I mail you a copy of the tape?" the compliance officer quite diplomatically stated. This is a real conversation I overheard. Now this is a dramatic example, and clearly the client was lying. But this issue was very rare; normally it was a simple mistake the client made.

However, sometimes when the client was wrong and wanted compensation that was under five thousand dollars or so, the firm would simply settle, pay the money, and close the client's account. The firm did no wrong, but decided to settle because the cost of litigating would likely be far greater than a settlement amount. While I fully understand that this strategy protects the bottom line, I often have wondered whether this was the best policy.

Some of you may view this as simply the cost of doing business for a brokerage firm. Perhaps you are thinking this unfortunate reality offsets ills the brokerage firms have perpetrated against investors who lost over the years. Well, I have served every type of advisory firm and person in my career, except for the commodity world, and I can tell you that every type of advisor has settled a case in which the consumer was in the wrong. I know of fee-only Registered Investment Advisers, who are fiduciaries regulated by the SEC, who have settled cases when there was no wrong done by them. They settled because it was perceived to be less costly at the time.

However, I strongly think that rewarding this bad behavior will collectively be harmful sooner or later. Regardless, the lesson here is not who is right or who is wrong, or how often one or the other is. The true lesson is to be open to the concept that you, the consumer, could be incorrect. If you are at least open to this concept, you may very well dodge your own bullet to your financial well-being.

How do you know if you are incorrect and your advisor is correct on a certain topic? The answer is fairly simple: ask your advisor to prove it in writing. Whatever the discussion is about a potential investment, tax strategy, or retirement question, financial advisors rely upon a vast amount of technical research and thought leadership created by sources both within and outside the firm. With printed information on hand, you can ask better questions and be better equipped to learn if indeed you are incorrect, or your advisor is.

If your advisor cannot support a decision with printed research from reliable sources, that is a huge red flag. Again, the vast majority of advisors provide you with true and quality service and advice, but you do not want to be part of the small minority who deals with a bad apple.

SO, HOW DO I TELL IF I HAVE THE RIGHT ADVISOR?

Now that you better understand how picking the wrong advisor can happen, you need to learn how to tell if your advisor is not right for you. In short, you should go through the questionnaire and process outlined in chapter 14. By going through this process, one of two things will happen as a result. One, you will determine that you do not have the right advisor at this point in your life. Or two, you will find your advisor is appropriate for you and you will hopefully gain a greater appreciation for the great work your financial advisor does for you.

There are some issues to consider as you go through this process, but are also helpful to think about now. Are you clear about what your true needs are? It is possible you are actually not aware of what your true needs are? For example, you may have a financial advisor whose sole focus is managing your modest investment portfolio. However, you may have extraordinary risk in your life because you have neither life insurance nor disability insurance, and with four dependents and many family members with a history of diabetes, you are wildly exposed. In this particular scenario, the odds are extremely high that you have the wrong financial advisor, as most advisors would not allow you to go uninsured (unless of course you ignored their prior advice).

Are you clearly unhappy about your current financial advisor? If so, why specifically are you unhappy? What exactly about your advisor makes you displeased? It is very important to be as detailed as possible and to write down the reasons for your displeasure. Be open minded about being reasonable, as sometimes investors can have unrealistic expectations of their financial advisor.

In the last market correction of 2008, some consumers felt their advisor should have better prepared them for a correction, and in some cases, even foretold a crash was coming. This is obviously unrealistic, and timing the market is something no one can do with success regularly. There are other expectations that you have that may or may not be realistic. Be open to learning that some of your expectations may not be realistic.

Some reasonable expectations including having a responsive advisor who returns calls and emails within twenty-four hours. Speaking with your advisor every day about the market is unrealistic and unfair to the advisor. Your advisor should be able to provide you with any information you request about your plan or your account or offer an opinion on a new investment or technique, such as Bitcoin.

CHAPTER 17

ADVISORS CAN MITIGATE OUR OWN BAD BEHAVIOR

Investors hire financial advisors to do the research, work, and spend the time performing the in- depth tasks we cannot do or don't have time to do for ourselves. However, there are tasks no investor can delegate to an advisor. Some of these actions are only completed by the investor but impact the investor's well-being, as well as the actual work the advisor is hired to do.

Actions such as spending, saving, and signing contracts are almost always done by investors, with the exception of the super-rich, who delegate these tasks to advisors and occasionally become victims of theft.

For the rest of us, exhibiting self-control with spending, being diligent with saving, actually signing the contract for that important life insurance policy, and many other actions can only be done by us. The advisor cannot brow-beat us into to submission or call us every day to make us be our best selves.

Although our financial advisors cannot be with us every day like the American Association of Certified Public Accountants' "Feed the Pig" ads, they do help us mitigate our bad behavior. Their ability to encourage better financial behavior is improving with technology tools that can automate certain activities and illustrate the benefits as well.

BAD FINANCIAL BEHAVIOR IS UNDERSTANDABLE

Bad behavior can take many forms and, for these purposes, there are several kinds of bad behavior. There is the kind that we are born with, there is the kind that is self-sabotage, and there is the kind that is, in truth, total ignorance. By ignorance, I mean the true definition of the word that we are simply not aware of an issue.

It is important to realize our own bad financial behavior is natural and understandable, and thankfully, wholly preventable and reversible. To begin with, good financial behavior is not taught in schools. There has been much written and said about the idea of teaching financial skills to our youth, and there have been and are to this day dozens of organizations that provide financial literacy classes around the country. The issue is they are not mandated or consistent, and as a result, most agree the effort has not succeeded yet.

Our parents, for the most part, did not discuss money and investing. We as a society do not discuss incomes, tax rates, savings, and certainly not in specificity to be helpful to others. Neighbors will excitedly discuss the relative virtues of the latest weed-whacker for forty-five minutes, especially if a beer is involved. We will debate the virtues of competing day care facilities in our hometowns, and who the staff is, and whether they are they treating our kids well. But discuss money? It's just not done. In the absence of formal education, the result is many will not have the basic financial skills to manage the simple things like a checkbook and credit cards, or understand mortgages and the like.

To add insult to injury, we live in a very materialistic, competitive society where social media and peer pressure creates a "keep up with the Joneses" mentality, and easy credit and the seduction of having five flat-screen TVs and three cars makes it very tough to have good financial behavior.

The following interviews, vignettes, and overviews of how advisors help consumers/investors are just a small sampling of the ways advisors can help investors overcome bad behavior. I specifically share seemingly incongruous products and services, but I do it on purpose. This illustrates how vast the offerings are used by an advisor to make the broader point that there is much that an advisor can do to help a consumer's behavior.

IGNORANCE: LIFE SETTLEMENTS

Consumers sometimes miss opportunities to improve their financial lives simply because they were unaware of an opportunity or strategy. There are even fewer opportunities for seniors to grow their incomes in retirement. For seniors, an unwanted, unneeded, or unaffordable life insurance policy can become an ideal opportunity to generate significant resources during retirement. The sale of a life policy is known as a life settlement (sometimes known as a viatical settlement). Every policyowner has a property right to sell his life insurance policy, and life settlements are highly regulated in over 90 percent of the U.S.

LightHouse Life Solutions, LLC is a life settlement company that purchases life insurance policies. Michael Freedman, the CEO of LightHouse Life, and the Executive Director of the Alliance for Senior Health Care Financing, a D.C. based advocacy organization, shared his insights about Life Settlements and how seniors can improve their post-retirement financial well-being through the sale of a policy. He also explained how Life Settlements can be a powerful tool for advisors to help their older clients, and these clients' families, realize the maximum value for life policies that are not going to be kept by the policyowner.

The vast majority of life insurance policies are eventually surrendered or lapsed back to the insurance company and, thus, never pay a claim to the policy's beneficiaries. When a policy is surrendered or lapsed, the owner receives little or nothing in return from the issuing insurance company. But, just like a car or a home, life insurance policies can be sold, and studies have shown that sellers receive tens of thousands, or even hundreds of thousands, of dollars in found money, which can be used to invest in their retirement, pay bills, or to finance immediate and long-term health care needs.

Individuals eligible for a life settlement own a life insurance policy with at least fifty thousand dollars in death benefit. The person insured under the policy is typically over the age of seventy and has had a change in health from when they took out the policy years ago. Potential buyers evaluate the policy and non-invasively review the insured's current health (through phone interviews and medical record reviews) to determine the policy's secondary market value. This appraisal, which is done at no cost to the consumer or the advisor, results in an offer to the owner and, once the offer is accepted, the seller receives the proceeds of the sale and the policy's ownership is changed to the new buyer.

It would be unthinkable to simply walk away from our homes, or to simply give away our cars and other assets without first seeking to maximize their value through their sale in a secondary market. Advisors advise and assist senior policy-owners with making the decision on how to dispose of this valuable asset in the policyowner's best interest.

Life Settlements are one of those tactics that many consumers generally are ignorant of, but the best financial advisors will not let this valuable asset go ignored.

PREPARING KIDS EARLY

The financial services industry has had a growing concern about financial literacy, especially among our youth. Numerous studies have indicated that the earlier people can learn proper financial habits, the more likely they will lead balanced financial lives. Financial advisors have been taking steps to help educate families on the benefits of early financial education, and employ various experts and products to aid in this education. One such expert is Nancy Phillips, the founder of The Wela Way, which is a program that teaches youth and their parents critical financial life skills.

Nancy, a kinesiologist with an MBA, went through a traumatic experience when she had a serious health issue while her children were very young. It made her think hard about what life lessons she wanted teach her kids, such as defining personal values, and other basic financial and life success skills. She sought out courses to help her, and when she could not find exactly what she was looking for, decided to create her own program from the research she was gathering. The Wela Way teaches kids and teens how to identify what is most important for them, including what kind of character they want to build and the power of saving, giving, and investing. Her program helps our youth feel more confident, prosperous, and responsible about money.

Advisors like Charles Massimo, President of CJM Fiscal Management of Melville, New York had Nancy make a presentation to his clients and their millennial children and stated, "Instilling proper financial behavior and habits at a young age has such an enormous impact as time goes on. In addition, providing a forum to discuss entitlement issues with the parents directly proved to be a great topic of discussion."

SOFTWARE APPS THAT ADVISORS USE

Account Aggregation

Account aggregation is a term for a tool that allows you and your advisor to see all your accounts in one place. Investments, bank accounts, credit cards, mortgages, insurance policies, and just about anything that is related to money can be seen on a "Dashboard" as it's called. When advisors ask their clients to use this technology, it helps reinforce better financial behavior. Of course, with any personal data, you need to be very careful who you give access to, in order to minimize the risk of identity theft or other types of fraud. Always ask your advisor for documentation on how his firm secures your data...and read that information!

For example, your advisor can see to the penny how much credit card debt you really have. You can no longer lie to yourself or your advisor. Here is a hypothetical example. You have twenty thousand dollars in total credit availability. Your credit card debt is twelve thousand dollars, and not four thousand dollars, as you told your advisor last quarter. That means several negative things. First, your payments are higher now, and automatically, you cannot save as much each month. Second, your credit utilization is now 60 percent, not 20 percent. What that means is if you were about to apply for a mortgage, your credit is a little worse, and perhaps your mortgage is now a little more expensive. This means even less savings because that future housing payment is higher. With this information at his or her fingertips, your advisor can both give better advise and guide you to make better decisions.

Client Relationship Management Systems (CRM)

If you work in a business environment it is highly likely that your company uses some form of CRM. They are software products that hold client information like phone number, email, physical address, and records of all communications with a client. Firms like Salesforce.com are very large and have hundreds of thousands of businesses using it. There are hundreds of firms like Salesforce, but essentially all client interaction is stored in these systems.

CRM systems can be programmed to automate reminders, and more and more advisors are doing just that. Automated reminders to send your tax records, to update your will, even to get your annual physical, are automated and make pesky reminders less uncomfortable (at least compared to a phone call). Automated reminders can help build better behavior, are less intrusive, and can be stored and reviewed at any time.

Private Equity Investment Platforms

For high net worth investors, investing in private partnerships can be an excellent way to achieve higher returns and have investment returns that are not correlated to the public markets. More and more advisors are subscribing to internet-based platforms for these investments, so the investments have the scrutiny and standardized platforms to conform to. This helps minimize the habit of investors putting their money into a vehicle that is not reviewed by a licensed, regulated, and supervised financial professional. For wealthy investors, sometimes they want to get deeply involved in a new opportunity and do not share it with their advisor. There is a great deal of psychology at play. It could be they don't want to be told no by their advisor, sometimes they don't want their advisor to know about other moneys they have, sometimes the advisors firm did not perform due diligence on the investment. There are certainly quality investment opportunities that are not on one of these third-party platforms, but having some third party—like an advisor or the platform itself—review them is simply prudent behavior.

Virtual Vaults

Advisors need many of your documents to review in order to give their optimal advice. To make this easier, a number of software packages have been created in recent years to make it easier for clients to send these documents to their advisors to review. We as consumers generally have a very bad habit of not reading the material we are given, let alone reading important documents that have critical details. By having a secure, online place for advisors to easily read documents, consumers can't forget to send them; this allows the advisor to read and discern if a financial related contract is a problem. In some cases, the advisor may find out that a mutual fund you invested in has mediocre investment performance and an unusually high expense ratio, which makes it an easy to decision to get rid of it and find a better fund. In another example, a life insurance contract you have may soon be increasing in monthly cost, and you did not budget for it. There are dozens of examples of practical reasons why have a common digital vault is a benefit to the consumer and advisor.

Polite Nagging

Having an advisor is also paying for someone to politely nag you to do the right thing. If you have ever had a trainer, a coach, a piano teacher, or a math tutor, then you know that sometimes they give you the message that you have not done your practice or exercises. Human behavior also drives us to not want to disappoint our coach, who simply wants us to be better at whatever endeavor we are engaged in. Over the course of time we develop better habits, or at minimum, become aware at least that we should be doing better.

Electronic Funds Transfers (EFT)

Many advisors ask their clients to set up an automatic savings plan using an automated transfer from a checking account to a savings account. This is in addition to all their retirement savings that may be auto-deducted from their paycheck. Advisors also often suggest bills be paid via EFT to avoid late charges, penalties, and negative events on credit reports. Human behavior is such that once an auto-deduction is set up, most people do not go to the trouble to change it, and they save every month without taking an overt action.

Monthly Retainers

Monthly retainers have the consumer benefit of reminding us each month we are paying for advice. We all want to get the value for something we pay for, so this monthly reminder is a beneficial expense to remind us to take that action that our advisor is telling us to take. It is also license to call our advisor when we have questions or to share an event with our advisor that might be an action item.

Reviews

Any reputable advisor will have regular, formal reviews with their clients. They will review your investment account to compare against last year's performance and the relative benchmarks. If a financial plan is involved, savings amounts, spending, and debt levels will be reviewed. Formal reviews force the investors to take a hard look at what they could be doing better, be it spending less, saving more, or getting that living trust set up.

Hand Holding in Emotional Situations

One of the most important times an advisor minimizes bad consumer/investor behavior is when markets are going into a tailspin. It is indeed difficult emotionally to handle watching the stock market—and your retirement fund—drop in value by a lot and in a short span of time. I have been through the two worst in thirty years, 1987 and 2008, and observed my own emotions and watched many others react to a market in free-fall. Notably, I had many people ask me what to do in 2008; these were investors in their forties, fifties, and sixties, and (one would think) a little more immune to the emotional stress of a significant and protracted market decline. Thankfully it is very true that an advisor will give an investor great comfort and will stop many from making irrational decisions during this time.

However, emotional and irrational behavior is not limited to just times of market drops. Really, we don't see that many drops of this magnitude during our lifetimes. There are many other emotional events in our lives that drive bad investor behavior unless someone intervenes. For example, in great bull markets, some investors get irrational and believe the market will continue to increase—and forget they always go the other way. This can lead to irrational behavior, such as the fear of missing out on a great ride and investing too much money at the top.

The investing bad behavior du jour of 2018 has been cryptocurrencies. I am not opining one way or another on crypto, rather pointing out the well-documented fact that many people have invested in cryptocurrencies without having any knowledge at all about the subject. This is precisely the kind of fad investment that needs a steady hand to opine on what to do. The pull of others making thousand percent gains in two years makes some people irrational.

The most common bad behaviors, which stem from emotions running unchecked, are those that happen from personal life events. The death of a spouse, a serious illness, being fired or laid off, a divorce, or even a sudden financial wind-fall, can drive people to make bad decisions. Most advisors have clients that have gone through whatever life event you are going through or have a peer that has had clients in your situation.

Financial advisors are not magicians and cannot force an investor to take any action unless the investor wants to. Financial advisors lament that, despite all the tools and techniques at their disposal, not all their clients take their advice. This is seen and heard at advisor conferences and events, written about in advisor trade publications, and I have heard it in one on one conversations for years. For the investor, however, if you truly want to improve your financial life and can take direction, your advisor will work hard to stop every bad impulse they are aware of.

CHAPTER 18

PERSPECTIVE: REGULATORY RECORDS OF ADVISORS, ATTORNEYS, AND DOCTORS

Compared to other professionals, financial advisors get a disproportionately bad rap. To quote the late comic Rodney Dangerfield, they "get no respect." Most people have a higher opinion of a medical doctor or a lawyer than they do of a financial advisor. Part of that higher opinion, of course, is that the educational requirements for medical doctors and attorneys are uniform, and more difficult or as difficult as the more challenging financial certification. Added to this is that there is no uniform financial advisor certification, and it is far easier to get a simple financial license than to become a doctor or attorney.

However, when examining the component of opinion that is driven by the transgressions of each of the three professions, then the facts do not support the public opinion. Paradoxically, financial advisors have a better regulatory record than both medical doctors and attorneys. Put another way, financial advisors violate their rules less often than medical doctors and attorneys. Because of this reality, this is another reason why the public negative perception of advisors is misplaced.

From publicly available data, here is how the three groups of professionals compare:

1. Seven percent of all attorneys are brought up on formal charges every year by their state boards, according to the American Bar Association.

2. Five percent of all doctors are sued by patients every year, according to the American Medical Association.

3. Only 7 percent of all financial advisors had an infraction over an entire career, well under 1 percent a year, according to FINRA, the SEC, and State Insurance Commissioners. The white paper "The Market for Financial Advisor Misconduct" by Egan, Matvos, and Seru published in September 2017 also establishes the infraction rate at 7 percent

WHY COMPARE THE DISCIPLINARY HISTORY OF ADVISORS TO LAWYERS AND DOCTORS?

In examining if indeed financial advisors are disproportionality perceived, I wanted to find some common dominator between financial advisors and other professionals. Publicly available regulatory history is a good common data point to use to compare the three professions. Admittedly, there are flaws in this because the three professions are so different and any comparison between industries has its limitations. However, negative reports that are disseminated by each of the three professions' governing bodies/associations is a good common comparative point.

Compared to those of doctors and lawyers, far more money and time are spent by the financial industry, regulators, and Congress to make advisors follow the rules. At the state level, medicine and law have only one regulator, and at the federal level, none.

Three regulators can govern financial advisors: FINRA, the SEC and/or state, and each state's insurance commissioner. At larger firms, there can be additional regulators, such as commodity and banking regulators. Simply, thousands of advisors are regulated by more than one regulatory body. Thus, oversight is much greater. With greater oversight and transparency, the odds of regulators or investors lodging a complaint increase. In fact, some regulators perform surprise audits annually.

FINANCIAL SERVICES' SELF-POLICING CONTROLS

Police departments have internal affairs departments to root out bad cops. The financial services industry equivalent is the compliance department. Its role is to protect the firm by following all rules put forth by the various regulators. Advisors jokingly call the compliance department the "revenue removal" department, because of the gantlet of rules, procedures, and forms that must be run.

For example, financial services firms' compliance departments closely monitor all outgoing communication including the use of social media. For the most part, the compliance departments at all the nation's financial services firms are strong and well-funded departments and are given the same respect as human resources and other core departments.

Law firms and medical practices do not have these types of supervision. Law firms and medical practices do not have named compliance officers to oversee the staff to ensure adherence to the various securities laws.

HOW INFRACTIONS GET RECORDED

Financial advisors have a higher probability to have a negative public record filed against them, yet interestingly, their collective records are better than doctors and attorneys as shown prior. For advisors, there are three opportunities to get something negative on the public record. First, a client can complain to regulator. Second, the compliance officer can lodge a complaint. Third, a regulator can file something negative. Keep in mind that regulators visit advisors and firms—in some cases, every single year.

For attorneys and doctors, there are only two occasions to get an issue in the public record: the client complains, or the regulator issues a report. There is no internal compliance officer level of oversight. Moreover, there are no planned annual visits to lawyers or doctors by regulators, so one would think given greater scrutiny, advisors would have more recorded offenses.

FINANCIAL SERVICES' REGULATORY CULTURE

Over the past twenty years, new and stricter regulations by compliance departments have changed the culture of the industry. And compliance departments themselves have become a vitally important cog in financial advisory firms' operating machinery. In today's heavily regulated securities industry, advisors literally fear compliance departments. It's largely because compliance departments and senior management fear the regulators be it FINRA or the SEC or their state.

OLD VERSUS NEW INSTITUTIONS

We respect and trust old and established professions, such as medicine and law, and are skeptical of relatively new ones, such as financial services. And that's one of the important reasons for the perception gap. Additionally, Americans hold in high regard the power of hard-won educational credentials. Conversely, compared to doctors and lawyers, financial advisors are relatively new in the public's eyes. Having been on the scene for about one hundred years, they haven't been sanctified by the vicissitudes of time.

FINAL COMPARISON

This chapter is intended to compare public complaints of the three professionals to illustrate that perceptions of financial advisors is unfairly low, using public complaint data. The comparison is a relative one, and not exact. For example, I have already pointed out that too many current regulators do not come from the industry and as such, either record frivolous infractions or miss frauds completely. If one assumes that all regulatory bodies have roughly the same inefficiency rate, then the mistakes of the regulators of law, medicine, and advice, are likely very close on a percentage basis.

A skeptic could opine that the regulatory data is artificially low due to nefarious actors or conflicts of interest at some level in the reporting chain, thereby making the advisors look better than they are in reality. It is always productive to be a skeptic; however, when considering that the comparative data are from associations of lawyers and doctors and not government bodies, one realizes that the relative numbers are what become important, even if the law and medicine groups also have too-low numbers.

To sum up, if consumers became aware that financial advisors are censured less than these other two professional groups, their fear of advisors taking advantage of them would be lessened. This should be bolstered by the fact that from most perspectives, financial advisors are more highly regulated on a day to day basis than these other two professional groups.

CHAPTER 19

ENTER THE ROBOTS

I will begin this chapter with its punchline: "Robos" as they are called, are a very new type of automated investment platform that allow anyone to invest even a tiny amount of money, and that program automatically provides some level of "advice" and invests in low cost mutual funds or ETFs.

Almost all of them now give the investor access to or through a live human being, which is very good and the way they should have been designed from day one. While an investor can and often does use them alone to invest, they are best used as a tool to allow human advisors to build bridges to investors with very small amounts to invest, making advice easier and faster to disseminate to larger groups of very small investors.

And now the history, which is important. When Robos began, most of their founders and management expressed disdain for live, human advisors and were not shy about it. Now most of them love human advisors. The reason is money, despite some of their pseudo-altruistic marketing. The reality is that the number of investors and their collective amount of money that wanted to be managed by these algorithms was not coming in at a rate fast enough to the satisfaction of their Silicon Valley investors, so they needed to additionally befriend traditional human advisors to help grow.

I and others in the industry watched Robos begin and get publicity in the advisor trade press, long before these Robos embraced live advisors. Pundits foretold of the demise of human advisors. I and others in the industry never thought that a computer program written by a twenty-something would threaten the human advisor business. Moreover, I thought that Robos, even if they were adopted, were simply a very bad idea.

There are many reasons why I think that a pure Robo solution is bad, and thankfully, the market has spoken and agreed with me. First and foremost, an algorithm alone is very bad for the investor. Investing is not science and it is not art. It is both. When art is a component of an endeavor, that means human involvement. Here is a very simple example: Someone decides to use Robo "x" and automatically invest three hundred dollars per month which goes into low cost index funds. Life goes on, then in eighteen months, the customer gets recruited for a new job with a 40 percent pay increase. What should the customer do? Stay with three hundred dollars per month? Increase the amount proportionately, 40 percent? Well, the customer certainly can't call the algorithm and pose this question, can they? This is just one very simple example—there are literally hundreds of if/then scenarios to consider.

Then comes the emotional state of the customer, and their ability or inability to truly implement a smart decision. A program simply cannot answer questions. Much more specifically, the computer program cannot look you in the eye and see by your facial expression that you are confused, lying to the system or lying to yourself, refusing to answer questions—and again, the list goes on. An algorithm cannot empathize and intuit confusion among the many other human emotions needed to give good advice; it is simply code written by someone else that follows a set of pre-determined rules. That is not true advice, and certainly not an adequate replacement for an advisor.

Investing is a very human and emotional endeavor. Just ask anyone who was invested in 2008, or pick your choice of market correction or full bear markets in the past. People panic in bear markets, and conveniently forget that bull markets don't last forever. It's human nature. In some cases, investing is something the person should not be doing at that point in life. In the case of high consumer debt loads where the interest rates far exceed market returns, a planner can easily make the case to use disposable income to pay down debt, and then when the debt is gone, invest. But the particulars vary from person to person.

Another reason pure Robos are bad: they are never used to state that there is a thing called financial planning or wealth management. Their marketing attempts to persuade folks—mostly younger investors—that the program is all they need needed. Wealth management involves many things, including investing, but a person's entire financial picture could be altered for better or worse by something other than a selection of mutual funds.

Finally, I did not care for the human advisor bashing that many of the early Robos trafficked in. Some of the marketing literally stated human advisors were bad and useless. I cannot fully fault the young founders and CEOs of these startups, as they likely were ignorant of the advice business. However, the venture capital firms that funded these startups propagated a false narrative and they should have known better. For anyone that has raised capital from venture capital firms, it is well known that many of these firms are less interested in the authentic long-term utility of the firm's service to the customer, and more interested in increasing their odds of selling their stake in the company in five to seven years. Let the next owner deal with the question of whether or not the company offers a beneficial service to the consumer.

I know that most human financial advisors are genuinely interested in helping their clients, as I have spoken with so many advisors and many clients of advisors. But observing the early advertising and rhetoric of pure Robos, their intent, despite other claims, was more for corporate growth. Everyone who could write a few thousand lines of code wanted to be the next Mark Zuckerberg, and venture capital firms wanted a piece of the action.

But now, all these firms think human advisors are just terrific because they can make money from them.

TWO TYPES OF ROBOS

There are two broad types of Robos: one, the kind that still hate human advisors. As of this writing I believe Wealthfront is the only one left. However, there is such a mad rush to create automated investment solutions—Robos—that almost every week there is an announcement of a new platform. One cannot hope to keep track.

The second type of Robo are the kind that embrace human financial advisors; however, it is important to note they break down into two sub-groups: those that started life hating human advisors and then became converts, and the group that started their corporate life embracing human advisors on day one. I trust the latter group much more than the former. However, human financial advisors are a smart group of people, and if a human advisor decides to use a Robo in the former category, then you will likely be just fine using that service.

SOME HISTORY

By most accounts, Betterment, started in 2008, was the first Robo advisor. Initial use was fueled by the fear and pain created by the Great Recession, mostly by younger investors who have a preference for a digital-first experience. In 2014, Betterment for Advisors was launched to allow human financial advisors to use their automated tools for small accounts.

Other firms such as Personal Capital, Blooom, Acorns, and SigFig entered the space and initially offered little to no minimum requirements and very low fees to use their service. Most of them later added live human advisors or began working with traditional firms like SigFig with its 2016 deal with UBS.

FUND COMPANIES, DISCOUNT BROKERS, AND TECHNOLOGY COMPANIES

As time passed, there was an increasing interest in automated investing platforms, and despite the very small amount of money being invested in them by consumers relative to the traditional money with advisors, other firms saw an opportunity to use these platforms to leverage their current client base.

For example, in 2015, Blackrock—the world's largest asset manager—acquired FutureAdvisor. In 2016 the large mutual fund company Invesco bought Jemstep, a Robo advisor, to increase its business with traditional financial advisors. That year TIAA acquired MyVest, which is a business to business Robo, meaning it only supports advisors and other financial institutions. WisdomTree Investments in 2016 made a significant investment in technology platform, and Robo for advisors is AdvisorEngine, whereby the WisdomTree ETFs will be incorporated into the investment offering.

Vanguard Funds, Schwab, TD Ameritrade, and Fidelity have all created automated investment platforms to serve their current clients, and in some cases to great success, as is the case with Vanguard, now the largest Robo advisor by far, with over one hundred billion dollars in assets under management. However, 90 percent of that money came from an existing Vanguard account, as opposed to investors who chose their Robo out of the blue. The key is that there is a human advisor attached to the service, for .3 percent, a lower fee than most other Robos.

You should understand that automated investing platforms are available through or with live human advisors, and this hybrid approach is advantageous as it allows you to get you to get both automated plans with personal guidance.

CHAPTER 20

HOW TO GET FREE FINANCIAL AD-VICE FOR THOSE IN NEED

Since you're reading this book, you probably won't find yourself in the unfortunate situation where you need pro bono financial advice. However, I am devoting this chapter to this topic because there are millions of Americans who are in need: born to poverty, victims of hurricanes like Katrina and Harvey, returning service members, cancer victims, and the list goes on. You as a reader may know someone in this unfortunate situation. My hope is you will share details about these wonderful non-profits with those who could benefit from their service.

One of the best-kept secrets in the financial services industry is the fact that there are organizations that will provide free, quality financial advice to people in need. I first learned of pro bono financial advice around 2004 when I was CEO of the Discovery Databases. I was told of The Foundation for Financial Planning by one of our clients because the Foundation was fundraising and wanted to approach financial advisors. My company had the largest database of advisors, and after learning about the Foundation's mission, we decided to donate the databases and marketing services to help them with their fundraising.

In the ensuing years I would often bring up the Foundation in conversation and I was always surprised when I met someone who had never heard of it. In 2013, I was on a New York press tour and meeting nearly every finance editor and many finance journalists in the major consumer press. In nearly every meeting, I would bring up the Foundation and was shocked that so many never heard of it, or even the concept that someone in dire need could get free help.

During that time, I had the privilege of meeting Terry McGraw of McGraw-Hill. Terry was in charge of, among other things, the firm's financial literacy foundation. I recall an interview of him on FOX discussing a grant they made to help educate New York City teachers about personal finance. During our meeting, I was shocked that he had never heard of the Foundation. I am not sure why the popular press does not write more about groups like the Foundation, but to be sure, there is much more we need to do to get the word out on these groups.

FOUNDATION FOR FINANCIAL PLANNING

The Foundation for Financial Planning www.foundationforfinancialplanning. org is the nation's only 501(c)(3) nonprofit charity solely devoted to supporting the delivery of pro bono financial planning. The Foundation funds other local non-profit pro bono financial planning programs. For example, the Foundation gave a grant to the Financial Treatment Initiative in Boston, which brings financial planning to at-risk families battling a serious cancer diagnosis. Another example: Little Tokyo Service Center in Los Angeles received a grant for their program that helps older Asian-Americans financially plan for later in life.

Since the Foundation's creation in 1995, over four hundred thousand people in crisis or need have received free financial guidance. It has awarded more than three hundred grants, totaling over 6.2 million dollars to national and community groups in thirty-seven states.

Here is one quote from a family that benefited from a program that was supported by the Foundation: "Without this program, I don't know where my girls and I would be. My financial planner helped me fix my credit, save over two thousand dollars and buy my first home. My life is forever changed." This quote is from a woman who is a nurse and a domestic violence survivor.

The Foundation works closely with the Financial Planning Association, the trade association of financial planners and all its state chapters to connect pro-bono planners to local groups. In addition, the Foundation has training courses to educate the volunteer planner on the special best practices of helping someone in need.

Jon Dauphiné is the CEO of the Foundation for Financial Planning (FFP), which is the nation's only non-profit dedicated to connecting volunteer financial planners to those in financial hardship. Jon, an attorney by trade, has spent most of his career at non-profits, notably AARP, formerly known as the American Association of Retired Persons. He has a deep interest in serving those at the low and middle-income level. What drew him to join FFP in 2016 was the passionate board and donors who are trying to inculcate a pro bono culture into the Certified Financial Planners' profession, much like the legal profession has a robust pro bono initiative industry-wide.

FFP funds programs nationwide ranging from organizations that address the resultant financial hardship from domestic violence, to returning wounded veterans to those coping with the impact that cancer can have on family finances. Recent research is also indicating that financial duress can have a physical impact, especially on those suffering from cancer, so the work of FFP and the local non-profits it supports transcends finance.

I learned a shocking statistic during my interview with Jon: 99 percent of domestic abuse victims are experiencing financial abuse as well. Financial abuse prevents victims from acquiring, using, or maintaining financial resources. Financial abuse is just as effective in controlling a victim as a lock and key. Abusers employ isolating tactics such as preventing their spouse or partner from working or accessing a bank, credit card, or transportation. They might tightly monitor and restrict their partner's spending. Victims of financial abuse live a controlled life where they have been purposely put into a position of dependence, making it hard for the victim to break free. Financial abuse helps keep victims trapped in the abusive relationship.

For most of you reading this book, you can't imagine being in a position where you are abused and not be able to get in your car, drive away, get a hotel room, call an attorney and the police, and begin restarting your life. But that is the actual situation of these victims. Many of the FFP recipient groups offer programs for people in these situations so they can get their financial lives in order in preparation of moving on.

Jon explained that generally the programs that FFP funds follow the trends in the population. There is a significant issue in the Unites States with financial illiteracy for example, ranging from too much debt to an inability to adhere to a budget, and the programs often address these very specific needs. Because of the highly personal nature of the need, very often there is a pairing of a live CFP to the person in need, and they may meet a number of times over the course of a year or more.

Britepaths is a group in Washington D.C. that was funded by FFP. This program helped a cab driver in his sixties who had almost no experience with appropriately managing his finances. One of his issues is he always had cash, giving him a false sense of his true financial situation. Over the course of his time being advised and coached, he was able to save for a down payment on his very first home. This was a dream of his that he never truly thought would happen.

My hope for the consumers/investors reading this book is that you consider making a donation to the Foundation for Financial Planning, as it is an extremely worthy organization, not just for the individual recipient of pro bono planning, but for society as a whole. If you know of someone in need, please refer the person to the link below that shows the various organizations nationwide that may be of help. (Because FFP is small and does not run programs itself, it is not equipped to assist individual consumers.)

http://foundationforfinancialplanning.org/our-work/current-grantees/

http://foundationforfinancialplanning.org/support-pro-bono/donate-now/

My hope for a financial advisor reading this book is twofold. First, I hope you consider making a donation. But second, I hope you consider volunteering for one of the associated local groups funded by FFP. FPA members can also frequently volunteer through their local chapter. The vast majority of advisors have a genuine interest in helping their clients, and what better way to expound on that desire than by helping others that are in need? Below is the link for advisors.

http://foundationforfinancialplanning.org/volunteers/

FINANCIAL PLANNING ASSOCIATION

The Financial Planning Association (FPA) is the national membership organization for more financial planners, including Certified Financial Planner (CFP) professionals. Through a close collaboration with the Foundation for Financial Planning, FPA and its eighty-eight local chapters and state councils operate a variety of pro bono efforts across the country.

FPA pro bono programs target underserved individuals and families striving to build assets and improve their lives but cannot readily access a financial planner on their own. FPA pro bono programs officially began with 9/11, although individual financial planners have been donating their time since the beginning of the profession nearly fifty years ago.

This organization has a great deal of resources and information to help volunteer financial planners understand how to help those in need, and very specific guidelines for each volunteer to follow to ensure the person in need is getting quality and compassionate advice.

Here are the local chapters that have pro bono website pages:

Austin, TX: http://chapters.onefpa.org/austin/pro-bono/

Central NY: http://www.fpacny.org/probono

Central OH: http://www.fpacentralohio.org/aws/FPA/pt/sp/probono

Central PA: http://fpacentralpa.org/Pro_Bono

Charlotte, NC: http://fpacharlotte.org/community-outreach/

Dallas/Fort Worth, TX: http://www.fpadfw.org/page/ProBono

East TN: http://www.fpaetn.org/pro-bono/

GA: http://fpaga.org/content.php?page=Committees

IN: http://chapters.onefpa.org/greaterindiana/pro-bono/

KS: http://www.fpakc.org/Committees/CommunityOutreach.aspx

LA: http://financialplanningnola.org/16

Phoenix, AZ: http://www.fpaofphoenix.org/Pro-Bono

St. Louis, MO: http://chapters.onefpa.org/greaterstlouis/committees/

Hampton Roads, VA: http://chapters.onefpa.org/hamptonroads/financial-planners/community-outreach-pro-bono/

Long Island, NY: http://chapters.onefpa.org/longisland/pro-bono/

Los Angeles, CA: http://www.fpala.org/proBono.php

MD: http://fpamd.org/about/community-outreach/

MA: https://www.fpama.org/

MI: http://fpami.com/content.php?page=Pro_Bono_Committee

OR: http://chapters.onefpa.org/midoregon/pro-bono-outreach/

MS: http://www.fpamn.org/consumers/pro-bono-outreach/

NY: http://www.fpany.org/page/probono

Northeast FL: http://northeastfloridafpa.org/16

Northeastern NY: http://www.fpa-neny.org/pro-bono/

Northern CA: http://fpanc.org/about/committees/pro-bono/

OR and S.W. WA: http://www.fpa-or.org/pro-bono-outreach

Pittsburgh, PA: http://www.fpapgh.org/

Puget Sound, WA: http://www.fpapugetsound.org/community-outreach

San Francisco, CA: http://www.fpasf.org/about/committees/pro-bono/

Southwest FL: http://fpa-swfl.org/content.php?page=Volunteer_Opportunities

Southwestern OH: http://chapters.onefpa.org/southwesternohio/pro-bono-opportunities/

East Bay, CA: http://fpaeb.org/about-fpa-east-bay/committees-2/

Greater Hudson Valley, NY: http://chapters.onefpa.org/greaterhudsonvalley/pro-bono/

Philadelphia Tri-State Area, PA: http://www.fpaphilly.org/?page=JoinACommittee

Tulsa, OK: https://www.fpatulsa.org/

UT: http://utahfpa.org/fpa-pro-bono-volunteers.html

IN SECOND CAREER, THE FIRST TWO YEARS PRO BONO

Anthea Perkinson is a Certified Financial Planner (CFP) and is one of the many planners who volunteers her time across the country helping those in financial need. Anthea lives and works in the New York city area and is a member of the pro bono committee of the Financial Planning Associations' (FPA) New York Chapter.

This is Anthea's second career in financial services. She had high level positions in product sales, but on the business to business side of the industry working for a global insurance company promoting the firm's products to banks, broker-dealers, and other institutions. In our interview, Anthea described that in 2011 she had an epiphany. She described how she was attending a women's top advisor conference in Santa Monica, California, and marveled how so many of the women described their work with individual investors. They shared that their career was incredibly gratifying in that they were truly helping their clients get out of debt, pay for college, or prepare for retirement. These professionals were not selling; they were serving. After returning from the conference Anthea decided to change her career, soon studied for and subsequently passed the CFP examination in 2012.

Upon completion, Anthea joined the pro bono group to get direct experience with consumers. She figured she would both be doing a good thing and get experience working with the retail side of the business. For two years Anthea only worked pro bono, helping those in need. She then joined an established planning firm in New Jersey, which catered to the typical higher net worth type of client. She realized her vision and her calling was working with average people who have real issues where her expertise can make a substantive difference. She now only works with average clients on an hourly basis, refers to other advisors any portfolio management work and has developed an expertise and a niche in helping those who have very large student debt balances. She said it was eye opening how many people there were, and how diverse a group it is. She has even worked with clients who are nearing retirement and have significant student debt.

When Anthea and her peers volunteer their time, all types of people from all manner of situations are helped. In New York City, there are various agencies that work with the pro bono chapter of the local FPA. Those in need could get help through the New York Public Library system, through the Family Justice Centers that are close to every family court, through homeless shelters, or even Habitat for Humanity. The skills the volunteer planners teach range from budgeting, to understanding a credit report is different from a credit score, to literally helping people track every dollar they spend weekly to see how they can save.

The work the pro bono volunteers do has literally changed lives. They range from helping someone in an abusive relationship get their financial independence, to finding and recommending no-fee savings accounts such as New York's Safe-Start Accounts, to helping people in low income communities avoid purchasing the wrong insurance and investment products. Anthea relayed a story about a family she was helping who had purchased a term life insurance policy and had mistakenly thought it could also function as a future savings tool for their daughter's college fund. Anthea could not tell if the family misunderstood the policy or if it was incorrectly sold, but regardless, had she met the family earlier, she would have saved them from a financial loss and heartbreak.

If you know of someone in financial duress, Anthea has several suggestions on where to refer people. First, most public libraries nationwide have literature from federal agencies like the Consumer Financial Protection Bureau, FDIC, SEC, and the Department of Labor on various personal finance topics. Secondly, many cities have programs such as they do in New York that provide online lists of pre-vetted, non-profits offering free financial education related to dealing with debt, purchasing a home, saving for college, and so forth. Finally, the Financial Planning Association has close to one hundred chapters throughout the country and many have a pro bono committee with local CFP volunteers.

HARD CODED INTO THEIR BUSINESS

The following two firms are examples of financial advisory practices that on their own offer pro bono financial help to those in need. I did not need to interview these two firms; they freely share their pro bono efforts right on their websites. I only share these two firms as examples of firms that care and as examples of the broader population of financial advisors who donate their time. Like all advisory firms, they are for-profit businesses that can individually only provide free advice to a small number of clients, so if you know of someone in need, please contact one of the national organizations already mentioned.

Abacus Wealth Partners is a financial planning and wealth management firm serving clients nationwide. Their mission is to expand what's possible with money and one of the ways they do this is by offering pro bono financial planning services. Anyone in need can apply online for a free personalized planning session lasting up to two hours, subject to the availability of the advisors. Through this process they're able to identify problem areas and determine the steps necessary to meet the most important life goals of the individual or family, such as obtaining financial independence, buying a home, or putting a child through college. The application, which is evaluated by their pro bono committee, can be found on their website. Each applicant is notified within two to three weeks if they were selected. Additionally, they provide pro bono planning opportunities in their Sebastopol community by hosting an event twice a year offering free one-on-one thirty minute planning sessions with an Abacus Advisor. The firm has a distinct vision for helping others which includes among other initiatives, donating 5 percent of their annual profits to charities, which past years recipients are disclosed on their website.

BOUTIQUE WITH PRO BONO

Chacon, Diaz, & Di Virgilio is a fiduciary wealth management firm with four financial advisors. Despite their size, on their "Who We Are" section of their website, is a pro bono section explaining that pro bono is part of their moral and ethical responsibility. The firm believes that in the financial planning profession they must address the unmet financial planning and investment needs of those around them.

FREE ADVICE IN TIMES OF TRAGEDY

Financial advisors and financial industry trade groups have a long history of coming together when tragic events occur to help those victimized. On October 1, 2017, a gunman killed fifty-eight and wounded over 480 at an outdoor concert in Las Vegas, Nevada. The Las Vegas Survivors Project www.lvsurvivors.org was created to provide survivors and victims of the attack with a way to find free financial advice from pro bono, fee-only fiduciary advisors. A number of the survivors qualified for a financial settlement, and as is common, understanding how to use the settlement was critical, especially if it was needed to provide ongoing financial support for a family. Forty-seven advisors from across the country volunteered to offer at least four free hours of financial help to those dealing with the tragedy and were required to take specific oaths to ensure the interests of the victims were put first.

There are a number of organizations that can help those in need, so as stated prior, if you know of anyone in need, please refer to the organizations listed. And please consider donating to one of these organizations to support the great work of pro bono financial advice.

ACKNOWLEDGMENTS

I have many people to thank, and I will do so in chronological order, in an attempt to not forget anyone. First, Tom Garrettson, my good friend from college who got me my first job at Shearson Lehman Hutton working for his brother, Tim. Working on Wall Street for Tim in the 1980s was indeed a valuable lesson. I remember those days like they were yesterday, and that early experience allowed me to move forward in my career. Next, to all the advisors over the years who were my clients and prospects, I thank each of you for the time and knowledge that formed the basis for my understanding of all the types of advisors across the country.

To all the consumers and investors that I met over the years, I deeply thank you for your frank comments about finances and investing. This book would not exist had it not been for an amazingly long and insightful blog post by Tim Ferris with John Romaniello as guest. John and Tim shared a great many details on how a first-time author can get their book published. I followed their generous advice to the letter and I am very grateful for it. I could not have the confidence in writing this book had it not been for veteran author and editor Bob Weinstein, who for many months helped me with my book proposal and showed me the ropes. To my literary agent Leticia Gomez of Savvy Literary Services, I am eternally grateful for your professionalism, candor, and hard work. To the Post Hill Press team, and especially editor Debby Englander, I thank you for taking a chance on me, for your hard work, candor, and expert guidance.

To my new friend and successful author, Kelly Kandra Hughes, I cannot thank you enough for all your help sending investors my way for interviews. Each of these stories will undoubtedly help others improve their lives, which makes the effort even more worthwhile. To the consumers, investors, advisors, and industry executives who I interviewed, I am deeply appreciative of your time and effort to help communicate your individual messages and stories. The collective points of view are broad, interesting, and informative, and will educate in a way I could not.

My friends, business associates, and colleagues both in this industry and in others, your enthusiasm for my project and your validation of the need for this book has been invigorating and has kept me going. To my mother, Patricia, and sisters Nancy, Vicky, and Alex, thank you for your moral support throughout the years and for this my latest venture.

Finally, and most importantly, to my wife Kara. I cannot thank you enough for your support. As a fellow entrepreneur and risk-taker, your moral support, understanding, and encouragement were invaluable in getting this book done. You endured many months of taking care of everything, allowing me to focus on the task at hand. The book would not be a reality without you. Thank you, my love.

REFERENCES

CHAPTER 1

- Wikipedia, s.v. "Bernard Madoff," last modified May 22, 2018, 11:53, https://en.wikipedia.org/wiki/Bernard_Madoff.

- "Frequently Asked Questions," North American Association of State and Provincial Lotteries, http://www.naspl.org/faq.

CHAPTER 2

- "Nearly Two-Thirds of Americans Prefer Saving to Spending," Gallup, last modified April 25, 2016, http://news.gallup.com/poll/190952/nearly-two-thirds-americans-prefer-saving-spending.aspx.

- American Institute of CPAs, "Less Than Half of Non-Retired Americans Confident They'll Reach Financial Goals by Retirement: AICPA Survey," April 12, 2017, https://www.aicpa.org/press/pressreleases/2017/less-than-half-of-non-retired-americans-confident-theyll-reach-financial-goals-by-retirement-aicpa-survey.html.

- "IRI Baby Boomer Expectations for Retirement 2017," Insured Retirement Institute, last modified April 5, 2017, http://www.irionline.org/resources/resources-detail-view/iri-baby-boomer-expectations-for-retirement-2017.

CHAPTER 3

- "New Study Available: Millennials Revisited," Corporate Insight, last modified October 18, 2016, http://corporateinsight.com/syndicated-studies/new-study-available-millennials-revisited/.

- Troy Segal, "Do You Need a Financial Adviser?" *Investopedia*, last modified December 22, 2017, https://www.investopedia.com/articles/basics/07/financial-advice.asp.

- United States Census Bureau, "Millennials Outnumber Baby Boomers and Are Far More Diverse, Census Bureau Reports," June 25, 2015, https://www.census.gov/newsroom/press-releases/2015/cb15-113.html.

- "Students & Debt," Debt, https://www.debt.org/students/.

CHAPTER 4

- "LIMRA: Nearly 5 Million More U.S. Households Have Life Insurance Coverage," PR Newswire, September 29, 2016, https://www.prnewswire.com/news-releases/limra--nearly-5-million-more-us-households-have-life-insurance-coverage-300335782.html.

- U.S. News, "U.S. News & World report Announces the 2016 Best Jobs," last modified January 26, 2016, https://www.usnews.com/info/blogs/press-room/2016/01/26/us-news-announces-the-2016-best-jobs.

- Bill Butterfield, "New Realities In Wealth Management: Hope Springs Eternal," Aite Group, last modified June 14, 2017, https://www.aitegroup.com/report/new-realities-wealth-management-hope-springs-eternal.

- Paul Sullivan, "Financial Advice Gleaned from a Day in the Hot Seat," *New York Times*, June 17, 2011, https://www.nytimes.com/2011/06/18/your-money/asset-allocation/18wealth.html.

CHAPTER 5

- Vanguard Research, *Putting a Value on Your Value: Quantifying Vanguard Advisor's Alpha*, September 2016, https://www.vanguard.com/pdf/ISGQVAA.pdf.

- David Blanchett and Paul Kaplan, *The Value of a Gamma-Efficient Portfolio*, October 25, 2017, https://corporate1.morningstar.com/Research-Library/article/831611/the-value-of-a-gamma-efficient-portfolio/. By permission of copyright owner II Journals.

- "Experience and Results," Financial Engines, https://financialengines.com/workplace/results.

CHAPTER 6

- "Statistics." Certified Private Wealth Advisor (CPWA) FINRA.org. Accessed July 12, 2018. http://www.finra.org/newsroom/statistics.

- "Investment Adviser Data." adviserinfo.sec.gov. Accessed July 12, 2018. https://www.adviserinfo.sec.gov/IAPD/InvestmentAdviserData.aspx.

- "National Center for Employee Ownership (NCEO): ESOP Plans, Stock Options, Restricted Stock, Phantom Stock, and More." How an Employee Stock Ownership Plan (ESOP) Works. Accessed July 12, 2018. https://www.nceo.org/.

- "National Center for Employee Ownership (NCEO): ESOP Plans, Stock Options, Restricted Stock, Phantom Stock, and More." How an Employee Stock Ownership Plan (ESOP) Works. Accessed July 12, 2018. https://www.nceo.org/.

CHAPTER 7

- Angela A. Hung et al., *Investor and Industry Perspectives on Investment Advisers and Broker-Dealers*, (RAND Institute for Civil Justice, 2008), https://www.sec.gov/news/press/2008/2008-1_randiabdreport.pdf.

- Department of Labor Fiduciary Rule https://www.dol.gov/agencies/ebsa/laws-and-regulations/rules-and-regulations/completed-rulemaking/1210-AB32-2.

- "2017 Scottstrade® Retirement Study Reveals Investor Confusion and Cynicism," *Business Wire*, March 28, 2017, https://www.businesswire.com/news/home/20170328006277/en/2017-Scottrade%C2%AE-Retirement-Study-Reveals-Investor-Confusion.

- Dan Iannicola, Jr., Jonas Parker, and The Financial Literacy Group, *Barriers to Financial Advice for Non-Affluent Consumers*, Society of Actuaries," https://www.soa.org/researchbarriers/.

CHAPTER 8

- "L.I. Businessman Dubbed 'Mini-Madoff' Gets 25 Years," *CBS New York*, October 14, 2011, http://newyork.cbslocal.com/2011/10/14/l-i-businessman-dubbed-mini-madoff-gets-25-years/.

- Wikipedia, s.v. "Harry Markopolus," last modified April 18, 2018 05:50, https://en.wikipedia.org/wiki/Harry_Markopolos.

- Wikipedia, s.v. "Libor scandal," last modified May 19, 2018 15:15, https://en.wikipedia.org/wiki/Libor_scandal.

- JP Morgan trader Bruno Iksil, aka The London Whale, made large trades in Credit Default Swap securities creating multi-billion losses. Wikipedia, s.v. "2012 JPMorgan Chase trading loss," last modified January 6, 2018 14:41, https://en.wikipedia.org/wiki/2012_JPMorgan_Chase_trading_loss.

- Martha Stewart was imprisoned for four months stemming from insider trading charges. Wikipedia, s.v. "Martha Stewart," last modified June 5, 2018 02:26. https://en.wikipedia.org/wiki/Martha_Stewart.

CHAPTER 10

- U.S. Securities and Exchange Commission Office of Investigations, *Investigation of Failure of the SEC to Uncover Bernard Madoff's Ponzi Scheme—Public Version*, 2009, https://www.sec.gov/news/studies/2009/oig-509.pdf.

- L. Burk Files, "Why didn't the SEC call the DTCC to verify Madoff's security transactions given that it was a very simple act that would uncover the fraud?" Quora, answered February 8, 2016, https://www.quora.com/Why-didnt-the-SEC-call-the-DTCC-to-verify-Madoffs-security-transactions-given-that-it-was-a-very-simple-act-that-would-uncover-the-fraud?utm_medium=organic&utm_source=google_rich_qa-&utm_campaign=google_rich_qa.

- "Investment Advisor FAQs," Frequently Asked Questions, NYS Attorney General, last modified 2018, https://ag.ny.gov/investment-advisers-faqs.

- U.S. Securities and Exchange Commission Office of Compliance Inspections and Examinations, *2018 National Exam Program Examination Priorities*, 2018, https://www.sec.gov/about/offices/ocie/national-examination-program-priorities-2018.pdf.

- U.S. Securities and Exchange Commission, *Fiscal Year 2019 Congressional Budget Justification Annual Performance Plan*, 2018; and *Fiscal Year 2017 Annual Performance Report*, 2017, https://www.sec.gov/files/secfy-19congbudgjust.pdf.

- Jane Lynn Owen, *Report to the California State Legislature: Broker-Dealer/Investment Adviser Program*, January 2018, California Department of Business Oversight, http://www.dbo.ca.gov/Licensees/Broker-Dealer_and_SEC_Investment_Advisers/pdf/2018_BDIA_Annual_Report.pdf.

- U.S. Securities and Exchange Commission, *Agency Financial Report: Fiscal Year 2017*, 2018, https://www.sec.gov/files/sec-2017-agency-financial-report.pdf#financial.

- Wikipedia, s.v. "Text messaging," last modified June 5, 2018 17:58, https://en.wikipedia.org/wiki/Text_messaging.

- Margarida Correia, "Merrill Lynch Advisors Will Soon Be Texting Clients" *On Wall Street*, last modified January 11, 2018, https://onwallstreet.financial-planning.com/news/merrill-lynch-advisors-will-soon-be-texting-clients.

CHAPTER 11

- Ron Lieber, "Yes, You Can Find a Financial Planner Even If You're Not Rich," *New York Times*, February 2, 2018, https://www.nytimes.com/2018/02/02/your-money/financial-planner.html.

- Andy Gluck, "NPR Reports on 'The Personal Finance Industrial Complex' and Says the Only Person You Should Trust with Your Money Is Yourself," Advisors4Advisors, March 6, 2013, https://advisors4advisors.com/marketing/public-relations/17299-npr-reports-on-the-personal-finance-industrial-complex-and-says-the-only-person-you-should-trust-with-your-money-is-yourself.

- Wikipedia, s.v. "Larry Kudlow," last modified June 6, 2018 20:23, https://en.wikipedia.org/wiki/Larry_Kudlow.

- Wikipedia, s.v. "Eliot Spitzer," last modified May 24, 2018 22:48, https://en.wikipedia.org/wiki/Eliot_Spitzer.

- U.S. Securities and Exchange Commission, "The Securities and Exchange Commission, NASD, and the New York Stock Exchange Permanently Bar Henry Blodget from the Securities Industry and Require $4 Million Payment," news release no. 2003-56, April 28, 2003, https://www.sec.gov/news/press/2003-56.htm.

- E*Trade, "E*Trade Commercial—Don't Get Mad," June 19, 2017, https://www.youtube.com/watch?v=yRGHG_C-dl0\.

CHAPTER 13

- U.S. Attorney's Office, Western District of Washington, "Former Seattle Investment Adviser Sentenced to 16 Years in Prison for Wire Fraud, Money Laundering, and Investment Adviser Fraud," March 13, 2014. https://archives.fbi.gov/archives/seattle/press-releases/2014/former-seattle-investment-adviser-sentenced-to-16-years-in-prison-for-wire-fraud-money-laundering-and-investment-adviser-fraud.

- Paul Sullivan, "The Cautionary Tale of an Investment Adviser Gone Astray," *New York Times*, November 16, 2013, https://www.nytimes.com/2013/11/16/your-money/financial-planners/the-cautionary-tale-of-an-investment-adviser-gone-astray.html?mtrref=www.google.com&gwh=522894595EBCEA84B80B9AB3D1F54EEC&gwt=pay.

CHAPTER 14

- "Global Investment Performance Standards," CFA Institute, 2018, https://www.gipsstandards.org/Pages/index.aspx put forth by the CFA Institute.

- "Investment Policy Statement—IPS," *Investopedia*, https://www.investopedia.com/terms/i/ips.asp.

CHAPTER 15

- Mekanism. "Charles Schwab – 'Curiosity Blind Spot.'" The Best and Largest Global Advertising Agency Directory & Creative Library - AdForum. Accessed July 12, 2018. https://www.adforum.com/creative-work/ad/player/34520199/curiosity-blind-spot/charles-schwab.

CHAPTER 16

- Most people failed to imagine Madoff and others can commit devasting frauds. Failure of imagination was one of causes for failing to prevent the 9/11 attacks, and should be a lesson we apply to other endeavors. Government Documents Department, and University of North Texas Libraries. "UNT Libraries: CyberCemetery Home." Great Seal of the United States. Accessed July 12, 2018. https://govinfo.library.unt.edu/.

CHAPTER 18

- Rebecca Riffkin, "Americans Rate Nurses Highest on Honesty, Ethical Standards," Gallup, last modified December 18, 2014, http://news.gallup.com/poll/180260/americans-rate-nurses-highest-honesty-ethical-standards.aspx.

- Adam Dachis, "How Advertising Manipulates Your Choices and Spending Habits (and What To Do About It)," Lifehacker, last modified July 25, 2011, https://lifehacker.com/5824328/how-advertising-manipulates-your-choices-and-spending-habits-and-what-to-do-about-it.

- Debra Cassens Weiss, "This Law Firm Will Spend More Than $25M in Legal Advertising This Year, Report Says," *ABA Journal*, last modified October 28, 2015,Law http://www.abajournal.com/news/article/this_law_firm_will_spend_more_than_25m_in_legal_advertising_this_year_repor.

- "White Paper: Financial Advisor Trust in Comparison to Other Regulated Professions," *AdviceIQ Articles*, 12 June 2012. Web.

CHAPTER 19

- Jessica Toonkel, "BlackRock to Acquire Robo-Adviser," Reuters, last modified August 26, 2015, https://www.reuters.com/article/us-futureadvisor-m-a-blackrock/blackrock-to-acquire-robo-adviser-idUSKCN-0QV1HU20150826.

- "Invesco Acquires Jemstep, a Market-Leading Provider of Advisor-Focused Digital Solutions," PR Newswire, January 12, 2016, https://www.prnewswire.com/news-releases/invesco-acquires-jemstep-a-market-leading-provider-of-advisor-focused-digital-solutions-300202958.html.

- "TIAA Acquires MyVest," TIAA, June 30, 2016, https://www.tiaa.org/public/about-tiaa/news-press/press-releases/pressrelease648.html.
- "WisdomTree Makes Strategic Investment in Advisor Engine," WisdomTree Investments, Inc., November 18, 2016, https://globenewswire.com/news-release/2016/11/18/891358/0/en/WisdomTree-Makes-Strategic-Investment-in-AdvisorEngine.html.
- Larry Ludwig, "The Rise of Robo Advisors—Should You Use One?" investorjunkie, last modified March 13, 2018, https://investorjunkie.com/35919/robo-advisors/.

INDEX

auditors 149
automated investment platform 201

Babbra, Amrinder 132
baby boomers 31, 218
back-tested performance 168
bad financial behavior 189, 190
bankruptcy 30, 74, 144
Barron Financial 66
Behavioral Governance 154
Benefit Concepts Systems, Inc 86
Bera, Sophia 35
Betterment 203
Betterment for Advisors 203
Billionaire 18, 126, 147
Bitcoin 188
Blackmail 131
Blackrock 204, 223
Blooom 203
Blue Ocean Global Technology 157
Blue Ocean Global Wealth 56
Boiler Room 91, 125, 145
bonds 15, 27, 28, 39, 60, 61, 62, 65, 66, 68, 78, 87, 91, 95, 126, 136, 150, 155, 164
Briaud Financial Advisors 72
Britepaths 207
broker-dealers 43, 60, 61, 63, 64, 65, 83, 110, 112, 116, 148, 167, 210, 219
brokers 14, 29, 60, 61, 62, 63, 70, 91, 92, 95, 97, 124, 126, 162, 185, 204
Buffett, Warren 76, 79

cancer 26, 205, 206, 207
Certified Private Wealth Advisor 77, 219
Cerulli 42
CFA Institute 76, 79, 86, 138, 157, 222
CFP 34, 35, 36, 37, 56, 76, 78, 85, 137, 157, 158, 207, 208, 210, 211
Chacon, Diaz, & Di Virgilio 212
Charles Massimo 192
Chartered Alternative Investment Analyst (CAIA) 79, 154–157
Chartered Financial Analyst (CFA) 76, 79, 86, 138, 155, 157, 222

ABOUT THE AUTHOR

Nicholas W. Stuller is one of the foremost authorities on financial advisors and is a respected and outspoken authority on the financial advisory universe. As founding CEO of two of the largest financial advisor database companies in the U.S., he has built the most inclusive web-based directories, which include deep data and intelligence on the two million U.S. financial and insurance advisors. The nation's largest advisory firms, mutual funds, and insurance carriers have relied upon his companies to understand the financial advisor community.

In 1985, Stuller began his career at Shearson Lehman Hutton (now Morgan Stanley). When he left the firm as a financial advisor, he began a successful career selling to financial advisors at firms such as Waterhouse Securities (now TD Ameritrade) and National Regulatory Services (acquired by the Thomson Company). Selling to thousands of advisors, Stuller subsequently built sales teams to dramatically increase revenues at the various firms he worked for. A gifted entrepreneur and salesperson, he went on to create unique directories of critical data on financial advisors.

Stuller is a widely respected spokesperson for financial advisors. He has been quoted extensively by the print and digital media, including *The New York Times*, Dow Jones, Reuters, and Yahoo, and has been interviewed by the broadcast media including NBC, CBS, PBS, and others.